Customizing Small Boats

Customizing Small Boats

ZACK TAYLOR

Winchester Press
Tulsa, Oklahoma

Library of Congress Cataloging in Publication Data

Taylor, Zack.
    Customizing small boats.

    1. Boat-building.   I. Title.
WM321.T38   623.8'231   81-10474
ISBN 0-87691-332-X   AACR2

Published by WINCHESTER PRESS
1421 South Sheridan Road
P. O. Box 1260
Tulsa, Oklahoma 74101

Book design by DESIGN FOR PUBLISHING, *Faith Nance*

Printed in the United States of America

1 2 3 4 5   85 84 83 82 81

Acknowledgments

Ultimately, one does not learn about boats by reading books about boats. But the hours I've spent talking about them is something else again. In my youth, my teachers were J. N. Van Deman and Vaughan Abbott. Both had the distinction of never being wrong where boats were concerned. Whenever I was foolish enough to differ with what they had told me, I always regretted it.

There have been many other teachers. Engineers at the outboard companies instructed us all — the boating press — as they changed outboards from small, loud, relatively undependable machines to the giant, purring machines they are today. Many plant managers have shown me through their factories.

My counterparts in the boating press instructed me; we've gotten to know each other well over the years. I have been kept on my toes by the worthiest of competitors — Bud Paulson, my counterpart at *Field & Stream*. We have been friends for years. Both of us are amazed at how many times, completely by coincidence, we have chosen the same subject in the same month. The late Jim Emmett had the boating helm at *Outdoor Life* for 37 years. As was the case with Van Deman and Abbott, I was also sorry whenever I disregarded Jim's advice and suggestions. When Jim retired, Bud and I enthusiastically welcomed his successor, Bob Stearns.

Lastly, I must thank my wife who has yet to object to the clutter (and expense) of a backyard filled with all manner of craft.

All these people — and many, many more — have aided, befriended, and enriched me. My thanks to all of them.

Contents

1
The Customizing Scene

In today's world you must be a specialist. It's no longer possible to be just a fisherman. You're a bass fisherman and fish out of a bass boat. Or you're a walleye fisherman and find that trolling backward is the only way to gain the precision you need. Maybe floats are your bag. Or offshore stuff. I know an angler who fishes for nothing but big saltwater kingfish and scorns all else. Blue marlin fishermen out of South Pass, Louisiana, run through hordes of tarpon and ignore them as unworthy.

Similarly, if you hunt from a boat, terrain, available cover, water depths, dangers, distances, and lots more will specialize your craft. Most hunting boats are duckboats — you need one for today's waterfowling. But plenty of moose get shot from vessels, and floating for deer and squirrels can often be productive.

For each of these activities, you can buy a boat that is generally suitable. After that it becomes a boat very specifically customized by you, to your tastes and your needs, and to suit only your fancy. More important, you've pretty much got to do the customizing yourself. The jobs are too small or too bothersome or, in some cases, too expensive to contract the work through a dealer. Maybe some aspects of it can be farmed out if you've got any money left over after paying for the boat and motor. But the small stuff, the final fiddling, is usually in your hands.

One thing the years have taught me is how fiercely independent is this army (navy?) of boat customizers and builders. Hundreds of hunters and fishermen have sent me their photographs and told me their stories about building duckboats from the plans I published in *Successful Waterfowling*. Almost every builder "improves" on the design. But *improve* is the wrong word. Each builder *specializes* it — refines it to meet exactly his needs.

And it's worth doing. You get what you give in life. Invest thought, time, and money in customizing a boat and the dividends start soon and last long.

For one thing, customizing adds to the value of the vessel at usually modest cost. Certainly a boat rigged exactly the way you want it gives you greater satisfaction while in use. And it's probably more productive. If you rig a holder for your landing net right at your fingertips, sooner or later it will slip under some old buster of a fish that would have gotten away if you had to lunge half the boat length to grab the handle, tripping over your tacklebox in the process. Another reason for customizing is that it's fun. "Believe me, my young friend, there is *nothing*—absolutely nothing—half so much worth doing as simply messing about in boats" is the classic quote from *Wind in the Willows*. Planning what you want to do, redesigning, searching through catalogues to find just the exact gear, and finally putting it all together are all happy times. True, boats being boats, a tear or two may intrude upon the blissful state, such as when you drill into the gas tank. But most of the tasks are pleasant ones and turn out well.

Supply Sources

You can't customize your boat unless you know what kind of equipment is available. If you're ever lucky enough to have your dreamboat designed by a naval architect, he will specify exactly the make and model of every piece of equipment in the vessel. His design really starts from this vast knowledge. For example, the dimensions of a certain engine—its length, height, width, and weight—will determine not only how large and exactly where the engine compartment must be, but also the size of the doors to the cabin so the engine can later be removed for overhaul without taking the cabin completely apart.

Similarly you might want to install removable rod holders on your fisherman. But you can't have this bright idea if you don't know that such holders indeed exist, and where you can buy them and for how much. If you live in a boating center, local supply houses *may* offer a great variety of equipment. Trouble is, 90 percent of us live in boon-docks sufficiently remote so the nearest boat supply house stocks relatively few items. They'll have rod holders, sure. Maybe several styles. But there are literally dozens of rod-holder styles. You want to know about all of them and be able to consider each. Opening up these options is the first customizing trick.

Fortunately there are excellent marine mail-order houses that have well-illustrated catalogues, which are your comparative shopper's guide to both what is available and price. All are discount houses (and I'll guarantee your local boat store never heard of a marine discount); all hold sales; and if you shop and wait, they'll send all kinds of bar-gains your way. Nor can you go wrong, because if your order isn't what you like, all the companies I've dealt with over the past twenty years or so will take their merchan-dise back and refund your money almost by return mail and without question. All now charge a modest amount for their catalogue, refundable with the first purchase. When you purchase something, your name is placed on a mailing list and you receive new catalogues (most are yearly) automatically and without charge.

There are probably plenty of other good marine supply houses, but the following are the ones I've done business with, and I can truthfully say I have never had a bad moment or been disappointed. In fact, just recently my son lost one outrigger socket for removable outriggers. This consists of a piece of angled pipe that holds the pole and fits into a base that is bolted on the boat. The whole set includes two pieces to a side, four pieces in all. My local boat store owner is a personal friend and hunting and fishing buddy, but all of his suppliers refused to break a set. To get the single missing piece I had to buy four — $50 instead of $12. To heck with them, says I. I sent the re-maining socket, along with a check, to Goldberg's and asked them to send its mate. They sent both sockets back — old and new — even though I hadn't bought the originals there. Here are addresses of mail-order houses for which I can personally vouch:

Goldberg's Marine, 202 Market St., Philadelphia, PA 19106. Toll-free ordering is possible at 800-523-2926. Outside toll-free, 215-627-3719. Catalogue: free; 227 pages; no minimum order. Goldberg's offers a customer service department for special prob-lems. They also are slightly more fishing oriented than the others, listing extensive lines of tackle, gear, and lures.

Defender Industries, 255 Main St., New Rochelle, NY 10801. Telephone 215-632-3001. Catalogue: $1; 168 pages with small illustrations. Defender is the best source for fiberglass materials, with a huge selection and explicit instructions and comparisons.

James Bliss, Route 128, Dedham, MA 02026. Telephone 617-329-2430. Catalogue: $1; 268 pages; good illustrations and slightly more product information than the preceding. No fishing tackle and not much gear. Specifically request discount sheet because the catalogue shows list prices only.

Bass Pro Shops, P.O. Box 4046, Springfield, MO 65804. Although the company is more oriented toward fishing tackle, no one equipping his boat for strictly freshwater fishing should be without the giant catalogue: $3; 268 pages. Discounts, and they have it all in rods, reels, and lures as well as cushioned seats, electronic gear, radios, etc.

Last but not least is Sears Boating and Fishing catalogue. Free. It won't have the variety of marine items that Goldberg's or Defender lists, and like Bass Pro, it is freshwater oriented. But good old Sears makes it so easy to buy, and the value is usually there.

Except for the Sears catalogue, all these are big, thick books. They require not just reading, but study. For example, a friend of mine admired a pair of Lucite rod-storage racks I had in one of my vessels and wanted to mount a couple in his own boat. I knew they came out of one of the above but I had to look and look before I finally found them.

In a way, the wealth of choice the catalogues offer is the basis of this book. For example, Defender offers the following cleats: open-base cleat in four sizes; teak cleat, three sizes; hollow cleat, three sizes; cast bronze Junior cleat; jam cleat, three sizes; sailboat cleat, four sizes; streamlined cleat, four sizes; dock cleat, four sizes (to 15 inches long!). Any of the others can dish up the same. I count twenty-five different kinds of outriggers and poles, with prices ranging from $1,598 to $139. With these books, you have access to virtually all the common marine gear built in or imported into this country. No single store could possibly offer such a stock and stay in business. And as you peruse this vast inventory, I hope you do not come to the same dismal conclusion I have: It still ain't enough.

2
Working in Wood

Wood is the most familiar material we have. All of us have worked with it to some extent. The techniques of drilling, sawing, and bending it are too well understood to recount here. What you'll run into when modifying an existing wood boat or taking it partially apart to customize it are a variety of woods, fastenings, and glues. Let's look at a few. Why only a few? Because the woods you'll find available at your local lumberyard will be very limited these days.

Available Woods

Oak is widely used for ribs (the skeleton of a boat), knees (braces where two parts meet), keel (the boat's backbone), and stem (the piece that makes the bow). Red oak in the north is not as good as the more common white oak. The good things about oak are that it is strong, it works well, and green, unseasoned oak when steamed can literally be tied in a knot. Bad things about oak are that it tends to split, it's heavy, fiberglass won't stick well to it, and it costs plenty.

Mahogany is a reddish, often exquisitely grained wood much used for decorations — transoms, paneling, doors. It can be used as a substitute for oak where strength is needed. It is also expensive.

Pine, the so-called sugar (white) or longleaf pine, is straight-grained, light, and strong. It is somewhat less expensive.

Fir is the least expensive of the woods. Houses are built with it. In boats it has a tendency to dry-rot (more about this later). In small boats where ventilation is good and/or replacement of parts is simple, it's probably your best bet. Most plywood is fir.

Teak is much used today for decorative trim. It is a strong wood but woefully expensive. It is very oily, so fiberglassing is impractical.

Cedar, or *juniper* as it is called in the south and west, is an all-around great wood — light, rot-free, easily worked. Glass sticks well to it. It is strong enough for stems and knees. It is often inexpensive.

Spruce is the lightest and strongest wood available (with some looking). It is so bendy that small sailboats use it for masts.

Plywood is probably the best material for an amateur to work in. It is a laminate — built up of light sheets glued cross-grain to one another. Standard sizes are ⅛ inch (hard to find), ¼ inch, ⁵⁄₁₆ inch (hard to find), ⅜ inch, ½ inch, and ¾ inch. Standard sheets are 4 by 8 feet, but 12-foot lengths may be available from your lumberyard on special order. There are many grades. Marine is clear on both sides, with no knots and any voids filled. Regular exterior is okay for boats. There are several grades of this depending on whether both sides are clear and all voids are filled. Shop yards as to price and quality. The one thing *for sure* you need to see on any plywood that you put on a boat is "EXT" (exterior) stenciled on the sheet in many places. Interior grades will quickly delaminate as the glues dissolve. I once made No Hunting signs out of interior plywood to save money and they barely lasted the season. Another peculiarity of plywood is that it will bend only one way, which must be taken into consideration in your planning.

If you have need for a specialized boat wood and can't find it locally, there is a fine old wood mail-order house that has it all, including 16-foot plywood sheets. They rip and plane to order and ship anywhere at "surprisingly low prices." A catalogue for 25 cents, "How to Select the Right Boat Lumber," will teach you more than you learned here. The address is: M. L. Condon Co., 278 Ferris Avenue, White Plains, NY 10603. The telephone number is 914-946-4111.

Nails and Screws

Regular steel nails will rust around the water, but most hardware stores stock galvanized nails that are okay for boats. There are a number of galvanizing methods. So-called hot-dipped are best. You can sometimes find hot-dipped galvanized screws and bolts. Salesmen will try to sell you cadmium-plated bolts and screws. They are okay, I find, even in salt water if you can keep a lot of paint on them and don't mind repainting often.

There are such things as boat nails. Old-timers will remember the blunt, headless boat nails of yesteryear. Now boat nails are round shanked with rings on the shank and a normal head. They are also called ringed or Anchor-Fast nails and as far as I know come only in bronze, an alloy of copper and brass, an excellent boat fastening under all circumstances. These boat nails can be had in sizes from ¾ inch to 2 inches. If you're taking a vessel apart and try to pull out a nail and the head comes off and you haven't moved the stem, it's probably one of these boat nails. You almost have to drill them out.

Brass screws are great for a boat because they never rust and are relatively easy to find in all sizes and because you can back them out after years of service and remove parts for repairs and alterations. But you can't use brass screws for underwater fastenings in a boat that will remain immersed because salt or polluted water will leach out the brass in them and the boat will dissolve. Use bronze. A good substitute and easier to find than bronze screws are stainless-steel screws. Always test stainless with a magnet before you buy it because some grades contain more steel than stainless. Brass can be used underwater if you fiberglass over it.

Brass screws and bolts in small sizes, boat nails, galvanized screws, bolts, ringbolts, and such are available sometimes at local stores and usually through the mail-order supply houses. A variety of other fastening materials can be bought from companies that specialize in fasteners. Glen L. Witt has a good line of standard fittings at reasonable prices.

Two such companies are I. T. T. Harper, 8200 Lehigh Ave., Morton Grove, IL 60053; telephone 800-323-4015; and Alvarez & Co., 135 South Bradford Ave., Placentia, CA 92670. Both companies have free catalogues that are very informative. Harper offers fastenings in nylon, titanium, aluminum, Monel, copper, silicon bronze, naval bronze, brass, and five types of stainless steel. While not every metal is available in all

The crisp lines of precision construction show in this shot of a boat framed up and awaiting chines and planking.

of the following, the catalogue lists exotics such as sockethead cap screws, hanger bolts, set screws, eyebolts, thumb screws, a variety of rivets, cotter pins, nut heads, and lockwashers as well as the standard carriage bolts, lag bolts, and tapping screws. And such variety in the old standbys! For example, brass screws in gauges from No. 2 to No. 30 and from ¼ inch long to 6 inches; carriage bolts in stainless, bronze, and aluminum in sizes (stainless) 10–24 (the last number is threads per inch) through ½–13 and in lengths from ¾ inch to 10 inches. And on and on.

The Harper guide to metal strength is educational and is reproduced with permission.

Typical Chemical Composition and Properties of Harper Marine Fastener Alloys

Alloy Designation	Alloy No.	Nominal Composition Percent	Tensile Strength (PSI)	Yield Strength (0.5% Offset)
Yellow Brass	10 A	Cu 65 Zn 35	68,000	43,000
Free Cutting Brass	14 A	Cu 62 Zn 35 Pb 3	55,000	25,000
Naval Bronze	11 A	Cu 63 Zn 36.25 Sn 0.75	60,000	31,000
Silicon Bronze	13 A	Cu 96.75 Si 3.25	80,000	38,000
Monel	21 A	Ni 67 Cu 31.6 Fe 1.4	97,000	60,000*
18-8 Stainless Steel	30 A	Fe 71 Cr 19	90,000	45,000*
T-316 Stainless Steel	31 A	Fe 68.5 Cr 17 Ni 12 Mo 2.5	100,000	45,000*
Aluminum, 2024-T4	51 A	Al 93.5 Cu 4.5 Mg 1.5 Mn 0.5	60,000	50,000
Aluminum, 6061-T6	52 A	Al 97.9 Cu 0.25 Si 0.6 Cr 0.25 Mg 1.0	48,000	42,000

* 0.2% Offset

Glues and Fillers

A variety of modern glues and gluelike materials make boat customizing a lot easier than it used to be.

Weldwood glue is a one-part powdery glue that you mix with water. It is cheap and easy to work with since it washes away with water before it sets. Keep a bucket of water or a wet rag close by when you work with it. Most hardware stores stock it, and most professionals build with it. I've had failures with it if I let the can stand around too long, especially in high-humidity areas. Also the temperature must be above 70° for the set time, which is several hours. The tighter you clamp it, the better it will hold. It doesn't work very well on oak or teak.

Two-part *resorcinol* glues are what I'd use for underwater glues in any substantial boatbuilding attempt. Elmer's has a good one, but it is expensive.

Epoxy glues are popular but are hell to work since it's impossible not to have sticky fingers, although acetone will clean it off. One advantage of epoxy glues is that you don't have to clamp parts.

New *silicone sealants* are finding plenty of uses on a boat. They're great for water-proof seams or "bedding" stuff. For example, if you put a rail on your forward deck, water will leak through the bolt holes unless you "bed" the part with a bead of silicone. Thiakol is an adhesive bedding compound used for underwater seams. GE, Dow Corning, and Minnesota Mining have excellent silicone lines. But I've found the silicones don't glue as well as the ads claim, and paint will not stick to most of them.

Wood dough and/or the plastic putties fill up my mistakes, such as holes drilled in the wrong places. A favorite technique of mine is to use part of the vessel as a sawhorse. This practice results in saw cuts where they shouldn't be and keeps wood dough and plastic putties in business. You can make a paste of Weldwood and sawdust for a surprisingly good and inexpensive filler. Marine Tex is by everyone's account the very toughest of all the patching materials. I sealed a gas tank on a car with it, apparently permanently, and a guy was telling me recently how he sealed the exhaust line of a Dutch barge when it burned through at a bend. Six months later when he left the vessel it was still holding.

Dry and wet rot attack wood and turn it spongy and, in some cases, to dust. Rot comes when wood never fully dries and is more likely in larger boats than open, small boats. But it is something you want to test for by probing with a knife, or better an icepick. If the point sticks in more easily than it should, watch out.

Any dry-rotted portions must be cut out and replaced. Plastic compounds are now on the market that "suck" into the spongy wood pores and harden and restore the wood. They are okay *if* you can apply the material as directed through many small holes. I once used it to restore the stem of a small sailboat that would have been extremely difficult to replace because to do so would mean dismantling the boat. But I could drill holes in the stem with the boat both right and wrong sides up and easily get the plastic into all the bad spots.

Wood Techniques

There are a number of tricky things that you can do with wood that aren't too well known.

The first is laminating—that is, gluing pieces together. Suppose you want to make a curved deck carling (the thwartship beams that hold up the deck). You can't bend a 2-inch pine piece, but you can bend a ½-inch piece. Bend two ½-inch pieces; then clamp and glue them together. Repeat the process with two more pieces and you have a 2-inch curved beam.

You can do this with plywood. While plywood bends in only one direction, very light sheets—⅛ inch if you can find it—can be forced into a compound-curve shape, and then you can glue additional sheets to achieve the thickness you want.

Another plywood trick in case the local lumberyard tries to hose you down for 12-foot sheets is to butt two sheets. Just join the two pieces and back with a piece of wood large enough to take the fastenings you are using. Cover surfaces liberally with glue and screw up taut.

Armor Epoxy

A new aerospace epoxy may offer another plywood plus. Called Armor Epoxy, it has great strength and flexibility when dry as well as tremendous gluing characteristics. Before members are fastened, joints are painted with the epoxy to increase holding power. Skin sections for hull and deck are temporarily fastened while fitted and faired, then completely painted on both sides, including all edges. The resin is absorbed in the wood, leaving a surface similar to a fiberglass surface. Permeation seals off any moisture that might enter and delaminate the plywood layers. The stuff is an easy-mix one-to-one ratio and costs $25 a gallon. One company that has it is Clark Craft Boat Company, 18 Aqua Lane, Tonawanda, NY 14150.

3
Working in Aluminum

There isn't any question that aluminum is the most difficult common material to work in. Even though aluminum boats dominate the small-boat classes — canoes, johnboats, and cartoppers — not many dealers really understand their construction or know how to fix them. Nor is the material readily available. You can't buy sheets of marine-grade aluminum at your local store as you can buy marine-grade wood and fiberglass. Marine-grade aluminum sheets or rivets, pipe, or rod are difficult to find even though they are manufactured in quantity. Many hardware stores stock aluminum rod, bar, and sheets, plus nuts and bolts. I've used a lot of these and they do have a place. They are easy to work with and, of course, don't rust. But they are soft and lack strength, and even aluminum fastenings will corrode in them in time. They aren't one of the many alloys of magnesium and aluminum that stand up in salt water. Actually you have very little way of knowing most of the time if any given piece of aluminum is in fact a marine alloy.

All this is regrettable because aluminum is a superb material with which to build a boat. No other material is as light, as strong, and as inexpensive. The hundreds of thousands of small aluminum boats in use attest to this. Although aluminum for big boats has never really caught on with the general public, a visit to the Gulf Coast will quickly show you what the stuff can do. Most of the crew boats that service the oil rigs are aluminum, and superb craft they are!

There is some forward motion to the aluminum story. Not long ago, hardware stores had never heard of the stuff; now most of them stock aluminum supplies. Aluminum siding and gutters have solved the paint problem. And it is a problem. Bare aluminum must be primed with a special primer that actually etches the metal with a slight tooth so that final paint coats will adhere. Bottom paints present yet another problem. You cannot paint an aluminum hull with an antifouling paint containing mercuric or cuprous metals — the most common antifoulants — because these metals will cause galvanic corrosion and eat through the aluminum. An inert toxic substance

11

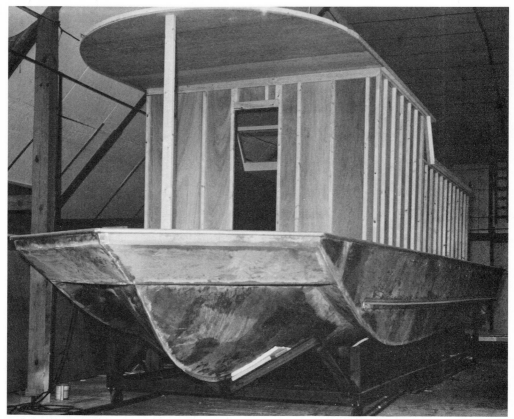

Polished hull of aluminum houseboat shows the inherent solid strength of this material. (Courtesy Monark Boat Co., Monticello, Ark.)

(generally known as TBTO) is equally good at inhibiting marine growth. However, it was so unavailable that Mercury Marine began to manufacture a paint line solely so skippers could get the substance to paint their stern drives. Today most companies offer TBTO bottom paints, etching primers, and complete instructions for their use.

Formerly aluminum welding was extremely difficult, a rare art indeed. Now new simplified techniques make it much easier to find welders who can handle the material.

There are several kinds of marine aluminum. The commonest is the 6000 series, which is form stamped into proper shape, then tempered with heat under carefully controlled conditions to gain maximum strength. Sheet and extrusions (molded or cast parts) are tacked together with rivets. This material is difficult to weld because the heat of the welding process reduces the temper, just as it would if you welded a knife blade. If the temper is not restored—another technical task—the joint will fracture not in the weld but in the weakened edges next to it.

Non–heat-treatable aluminum in the 5000 series lacks the strength of the tempered material, but greater thickness and extra frames can regain satisfactory strength, and this material can easily be welded.

A further welding hazard is posed by neoprene seals that are sometimes used to ensure watertightness between the keel and the bottom. Grumman canoes, which dominate the canoe market, are built this way. Heating burns up the neoprene, which cannot then be replaced without removing the entire keel.

Aluminum skin thickness in boats in popular uses varies from 0.023 inch in Sportspal canoes to 0.80 inch used in large runabouts. Most canoes and johnboats have a skin thickness in the 0.050 range.

If your reaction to all this is "Who needs it?" you are part of the crowd. It is just these factors that frighten people away from using aluminum. Do not be disheartened. Today most steel supply houses stock aluminum sheets and pipes in most sizes and shapes, and at least one I talked to stocked both the 6000 and 5000 series. Whatever other kind of materials you need — tubing for a Bimini tower, for example — can probably be gotten fairly easily. Almost all airplanes are framed and skinned with aluminum. Skin sheets, rivets in all sizes, and, if you are ingenious, all manner of support beams and bulkheads are readily available at the closest airport.

So the *real* aluminum story is that what at first looks fairly dark brightens considerably with a longer look. Aluminum in all gauges can be drilled with regular drills and cut with saber saws with hacksaw blades. Epoxy plastic pastes stick to it, as does epoxy resin. Brass or bronze fastenings attached to aluminum will react galvanically and corrode — slowly in the air, quickly under water — so stainless-steel fittings are commonly used. These are light, strong, and reasonably priced. Stainless-steel fittings were also hard to find at one time, but now most hardware stores have good supplies. All the aluminum fasteners I've found at hardware stores are too weak for most holding purposes. But they don't have to be. The I. T. T. Harper Company lists the following aluminum parts in alloys (whose strength is shown in the chart on p. 8): hex-head bolts, carriage bolts, all manner of nuts, wing nuts, cap nuts, machine screws, various sizes of threaded rod, lockwashers, flat washers, rivets ⅛ through ¼ and from ¼ inch to 2 inches in length. In stainless steel, Harper has all the above plus sockethead cap screws, lag bolts, eyebolts, set screws, wood screws, tapping screws, studs, cotter pins, and common nails. Harper's guide (in the previous chapter) to the strength of its fastening materials shows you how the various materials compare.

Aluminum Repairs

RIVETS. The most common aluminum customizing is often a result of dire necessity: The rivets in your boat work loose and start to leak. What you must do is rerivet with one size larger. Cut the head off the defective rivet(s) with a cold chisel and punch out the stem. If you can't chop off the head, you may have to drill out the rivet. You may need to redrill to make sure that the new rivets are exactly the right fit.

You can do a lousy-looking, but okay, holding job with two hammers. Get as heavy a hammer as you can and have someone hold it against the head. With a ball-peen hammer, peen the stem with strong, fast taps. This will tend to distort the head and bend the shank of the rivet slightly. What you really need is a head set. You can make both a head set and bucking bar from a piece of scrap iron or an old railroad spike. Drill the iron as close to the size of the head as you can — same diameter, same depth. Do approximately the same with the bucking bar. Now have someone hold the head set over the rivet head, put the hole of the bucking bar against the stem, and hit it with sharp blows. It won't do any harm to practice this a few times.

PATCHES. If you've got a hole or tear in an aluminum hull and can't find an aluminum welder, cut a rectangular patch of aluminum to fit over it. Make the patch about 1½ inches wider than the tear in all directions and plan to run a line of rivets around the edge, ⅜ inch in from the edge and about 1 inch apart. Before you drill the rivet holes, drill a hole in each end of the crack or tear to prevent the crack or tear from continuing. Drill the holes for the rivets in the hull and the patch. Coat the bearing surfaces with silicone sealer and attach the patch using the above riveting techniques.

DENTS. Aluminum hulls often dent but don't tear. Pound the dents out the way you would on a car. A heavy hammer smacking against a piece of two-by-four works better than a rubber hammer. If you've got a big dent or want an aesthetic job, you might inquire if a local auto body shop will do the job. They are used to repairing dents, but they might not be used to aluminum.

Aluminum and Wood

If the thought of working in aluminum intimidates you, there's an easy way out. Use the Zack Taylor, or coward's, way out by bolting a wood strip to an existing hull with stainless bolts. Then continue building in wood.

Let's say you want to install a casting deck in the bow of a small skiff. You could rivet supports into the keel and sides and lay in an aluminum platform. No maintenance, no rot, not much weight. But aluminum intimidates you. Go the wood way. Bolt a strip of wood to the hull so that a plywood plate can be cut to sit on it. Wooden supports under the platform rest on the keel. Glue and screws tighten the whole thing. I've used this technique many times, and it is a favorite of the barge-blind crew.

4
Working in Fiberglass

Fiberglass is marvelous stuff. Working with it is a snap. It is by far the easiest boat-building material to use, requiring the fewest skills. Almost none of the craftsmanship needed to build wood boats lingers on in this age of plastics. It took years of apprenticeship to learn to be a shipwright in the era of wood boatbuilding. Fiberglass production techniques can be learned in hours.

Plastic resin and glass cloth are much more easily obtained than, say, marine aluminum. Any lumberyard or hardware store carries all the plastic components needed to build a large cruiser. Sears, for example, carries a fairly complete fiberglass line directed toward boat needs. Defender Industries carries everything a plastic boatbuilder could conceivably require — for example, glass cloth in weights per square yard of 4, 6, 7.5, 10, 12.5, and 20 ounces and tapes from 1½ to 12 inches wide. Defender also has materials for other exotic building techniques such as substituting Vectra, Xynole-polyester, and Kevlar for the fiberglass cloth.

I think it is safe to generalize that most people aren't fully aware of the simplicity of fiberglass. It is really easy to build a plastic-and-glass boat from scratch. And certainly customizing one to your own desires is well within the ability of any boat owner.

But nothing is perfect. Some people are allergic to the styrene fumes in the resin and to the acetone that is used to clean up. Heart rate and breathing can be affected. The most common reaction is itching. Some people can't tolerate the slightly sweet smell of the resin. The smell is all-pervasive and lingers the way the old fish-oil paint smells did.

Both polyester and epoxy resins are heat sensitive, with best working temperatures from 70° to 80°. Fiberglass is extremely sticky. Keeping clean during a project is difficult, and cleanup is not an easy task. While drying (curing) times can be varied by varying the amount of hardener, as with cement, once the chemical reaction starts, no force can stop it. All of us have experienced the famed "fiberglass frantics" — that is, slopping the goo on as fast as possible because you can feel the brush gradually freezing in the can. The resins in fiberglass are highly flammable. It actually has a kindling

15

point below most woods, and it burns hotter and faster. Heat is a product of curing, and the resin can actually reach flammable temperatures without adequate air cooling. There are fire-retardant additives that can reduce the flammability. Uniflite boats, originally built for Vietnam service, feature fire-retardant glass.

But on balance, the charm of fiberglass easily overshadows its darker side. The thing I like best about fiberglass is that it does what it's supposed to do. In this day of highly touted "miracle" substances that promise so much more than they deliver, plastic stands out. It works. Fiberglass is forgiving. If you make a mistake, grind it away and try again. I have a friend who used fiberglass on a lapstraked skiff back in the early days when it was new to us all. He didn't know about mixing in the catalyst. "It doesn't harden," he said when he called me for help. We both stared at the gooey bottom. What to do? None of the books offered advice. Finally we decided nothing could be lost by mixing another batch of resin with extra hardener in it and slurping it on as fast as possible. It worked perfectly.

The ease of fiberglass construction shows here. Cloth is smoothed into the mold and wetted out with resin. In a matter of hours the hull is formed.

Fiberglass can be cut with hand or power saws. Ordinary drills go through it easily. Disc sanders with heavy-toothed sandpaper grind it away quickly, allowing the stuff to be easily shaped. Fiberglass will never rot. Sunlight does not deteriorate it. It is impervious to most chemicals. Neither heat nor cold affects its strength. It will be important to our demands that a plastic boat can drive through ice that would slice a wood boat to shreds. It can be painted and/or restored with no special knowledge of materials. It is incredibly strong and springy, and it fashions easily into the curvy sections that make for beautiful boats. Properly used it will last apparently indefinitely. The Coast Guard recently cut a panel out of the bottom of one of its earliest plastic boats. It had seen twenty years of service, part of it on the Houston, Texas, ship channel, one of the nation's most polluted bodies of water. The section had even greater strength than when it was built.

With wood boats, repairs were always difficult and expensive and usually required master craftsmanship. Fiberglass boats are a cinch to repair, which means they are supersimple to customize as well. It's possible to build a poor fiberglass boat. It's done all the time. But you can take a clunker and with more and better materials, stiffening, and so forth, remake the craft into a strong, long-lasting vessel.

Because of many modern materials, I believe that the "good old days of boating" are here now. Fiberglass is a large part of the reason why.

Fiberglass construction is much like concrete work. The plastic corresponds to the sand-cement mixture; the glass cloth in various forms acts like the steel reinforcing rods that give concrete its great strength. Plastic without the reinforcing of the inner skeleton lacks strength. Some people paint the inside of boats with plain plastic, but they would do as well with cheaper paint because resin alone sticks poorly and adds not a whit of strength. Like concrete, plastic continues to get harder throughout its life. In a proper mixture, it never reaches the point at which it cracks or weakens in any way, nor will it turn brittle in anything less than arctic temperatures. Let's take a quick look at the various available forms.

Skeletal Materials

The skeletal sections are usually made of spun glass. (Don't ever wash any clothes in the same water as any fiberglass materials—curtains, for example. The tiny glass fibers will permeate the cloth and act like itching powder.) The cloth is often woven like the cloth in your shirt, in the weights mentioned. The heavier the weight, the stronger. The mat is short strands of fibers pressed together. Mat isn't as strong as cloth, but it is smooth and makes a good surfacing material and/or filler. Strongest of all are the roving, thick fibers woven in a basketweave. If you are going to buy a fiberglass boat and don't see this basketweave in the hull, make the salesman explain why it is not there.

There are other skeletal materials. Glass cloth doesn't stretch, and if you are going to cover a round section such as a ball, you must carefully cut pieces to fit and be flat. *Vectra* and *Xynole polyester* do stretch and can be fitted more easily over curvy surfaces. If you want to cover a canoe, stretch Xynole over it, stapling it in place with stainless-steel, Monel, or bronze staples. When the skin is completely flat, saturate it with resin. *Kevlar* is another fairly new reinforcing agent, stronger than steel for its weight and without stretch.

Resins

There are two kinds of readily available resins, *polyester* and *epoxy*. Both are inert until you mix a catalyst, also called hardener, with them, at which point they start to cure. Depending on the temperature and amount of hardener, curing time can be controlled. Heat speeds it up, cold retards it. Even in subzero temperatures, the stuff will eventually cure, however.

Polyester resin will lift paint like a paint remover. Use cheap brushes with unfinished handles for the stuff. Polyester doesn't stick as well as epoxy, which is like epoxy glue. Use epoxy over metal or on oak or mahogany. Epoxy is stronger than polyester and costs about twice as much. Its adhesion is greater. The stuff you paint on is much like epoxy glue. It is possible to lay a first layer of epoxy for adherence and strength and then put polyester coats or layers over it. Both materials are absorbed into the skeletal material and need several coats to build up to maximum strength.

There is no set way to apply the stuff. For small jobs, paint the goo on with cheap paintbrushes. Bigger jobs are easier if you use a roller, which tends to force the resin into the mat or cloth and spreads it quickly. You can spread the stuff around on very small jobs with paint stirrers or popsicle sticks. Use throwaway cans, paper cups, or buckets. If the stuff affects your skin, wear inexpensive plastic gloves.

Thin the goo with styrene, thicken it with thickening powder. Acetone will clean it off brushes and hands. Resin on clothes is worse than paint; it really cannot be washed out. On bigger jobs have newspapers handy because the stuff gets on your shoes and then lifts the paper. I'm sure both resins are toxic if eaten and irritating to the eyes, but as far as I know, neither has ever presented any problems on a practical level.

Foams

Fiberglass by itself sinks, and boats must be kept afloat with added foam flotation that comes in various forms. Dow-Corning Styrofoam is the most common. It is what is found under the seats of small aluminum boats. Its advantages are that it is inexpensive—a "plank" that is 20 inches by 9 feet by 7 inches deep is $36—readily available, and long-lasting if it is not exposed to handling. It is easily cut into shapes. A cubic foot will float 50 to 60 pounds. The disadvantages of Styrofoam include the following. Gasoline, oil, and polyester resin will dissolve it. Rats, mice, and muskrats will chew it up to make nests. It gradually absorbs water, adding weight. It cannot be fitted into other than squarish areas and must be covered with glass cloth and epoxy or an aluminum shield for durability.

Polyvinylchloride, or PVC foam, is much tougher, won't absorb water, and floats 60 to 70 pounds per cubic foot. However, it is much more expensive. PVC is nonaging and inert; gas, oil, and chemicals won't dissolve or weaken it. A sheet that is ¼ inch by 36 inches by 72 inches costs about $30.

Foam-in-place is a two-part polyurethane foam that can be mixed together in liquid form and poured into areas where it foams and fills and hardens. It is useful for utilizing out-of-the-way spots to add to the vessels flotation. It has an adhesive quality and after hardening is gas- and oil-resistant. It has low water and thermo permeability.

Fiberglass over Wood

Fiberglassing a wood boat to stop leaks, strengthen it, or afford ice protection is generally considered the least successful use of fiberglass. The problem is adhesion. The glass pulls away from the wood if all conditions are not met. In this case the job goes for naught. Yet fiberglassing a wood boat is widely practiced for several reasons. It stiffens up an old boat tremendously, although if a wood boat is "working" — that is, flexing — it should be stiffened internally before applying the fiberglass.

The soundest reason for fiberglassing is to make the boat watertight. Many an old wood boat is sound, but the seams simply won't hold caulking. Sometimes you can use a seam compound — Thiokol is the best — to make them tight. But often there are so many leaks to stem that a sheet of fiberglass over the hull below the waterline is the best way. Another reason for fiberglassing duckboats is that fiberglassing allows the boat to run through ice without harm.

There are a number of rules for this business that are broken with peril.

Any wood must be absolutely sound. If there is dry or wet rot, the plastic won't adhere. You'll have to replace bad areas with new wood — not too demanding, since you don't need to make joints watertight. Or you might saturate the rot with "Git Rot" or a similar absorbing plastic. The first stipulation, then, is a sound base.

The wood must be absolutely dry. It can contain no moisture. Store the boat in a garage or turn it over and lay a tarp over the bottom. If you can put the boat in a heated area, so much the better. If a boat is really water-soaked, as it might be at the end of a season, let it dry for at least two weeks before you start working on it.

The wood must contain no oil. If any area has ever had oil spilled on it, the wood must be sanded away until sound, nonoily wood is met.

What kind of wood is important? Soft woods such as cedar and pine hold the cloth best. Plywood also holds well. Oak and mahogany are oily enough that adhesion is always a problem; use epoxy for its greater adhesion for at least the first coat. Another trick is to sheathe oak or mahogany parts with a light sheet of plywood and glass it. Teak is generally considered too oily for any glass to stick to it.

Epoxy resin won't react in any way with paint. Polyester, however, will lift it like paint remover. If you have good paint adhesion, you can epoxy over it. The paint's adhesion is probably as strong as the fiberglass's bond. Polyester presents problems: you must remove all paint. If you've got a new boat, of course, you have bare wood to start with. If the wood has been painted, you must sand it off because almost all paint removers leave a waxy film that can't be washed off and that will prevent the glass from sticking. Get a disc sander and the heaviest sandpaper you can find. This isn't much fun, especially if you are removing bottom paint. Some kinds are poisonous if inhaled.

With the paint off, cover the wood and let it dry completely for at least a week. Mix enough resin to coat the wood, paint it on, and let it set up. You want to avoid a "resin-starved" condition. On open-pored woods like cedar, fir, and some pine, the resin will go on and then be slowly absorbed into the wood so that there isn't enough actually adhering to the glass fibers. Letting one coat set avoids this condition.

The next step is to lay the glass on without having any voids or bubbles between the wood and the glass. Fiberglass cloth doesn't go around sharp corners well or into sharp grooves. Round off the edges and/or fill the grooves with fiberglass putty. The lighter weight the glass, the easier it will fill these voids. If you can, remove the keel and bolt it back on after the glass sets up. If you are covering the wood solely to prevent leaks, you can use a lightweight cloth. If you want to add to the strength of the boat, a heavier grade is necessary. You may want several layers. Most of the glass cloth you'll find in hardware stores is 10 ounce, and this is a good compromise grade for both qualities. If you have an exceptionally curvy surface to cover, use the stretchy Xynole cloth.

With the cloth in place, saturate it with resin. You can brush it on out of a can or squeegee with a piece of rubber. Try and get the buildup approximately the same everywhere. If you must work on a vertical surface, there are agents to add to the resin that increase its viscosity to the point where the stuff won't run or sag.

Your eye is the determining factor here. The resin darkens the cloth. You can read by the light and dark spots if every place has the right amount. If bubbles get in the cloth and lift it up, cut the cloth with a razor blade to release the trapped air and lay the cloth flat with a daub of resin on it. If you have any trimming to do, there is a stage in the curing when the glass is hard enough to stand up to ordinary scissors, but not hard enough that it will turn the blades. If you trim at this point it's easier. After the resin hardens, you'll have to saw to trim.

When the resin sets up, examine your work for bubbles or voids. If you have these (and you probably will), get out your grinder and remove all glass back to where you have good adherence. Then cut a new piece slightly larger than the bare spot and resaturate. If the rough edges bother you, they can be sanded smooth after the plastic hardens. When you've got everything the way it should be — no spots where adherence isn't good — give the boat a final coat. Wait a couple of days before launching. Keep the boat out of the rain in all this because rain may turn relatively new (a couple of days old) plastic milky. When cured, the bottom can be painted with any antifouling bottom paint. Sears has about the cheapest, and it is really good stuff.

I've followed this procedure with four boats and had no delaminating problems. But all the boats were cedar or plywood. In the cedar boat the stem was oak, and I polyestered to it and epoxied the stem. It stuck, but just barely. However, newer techniques for fiberglassing wood now suggest that the glass cloth should always be physically fastened to the wood as well. Use ring nails and space them 4 to 6 inches apart. On smaller jobs staplers with Monel, stainless, or bronze staples can do the job faster. Personally, I'd staple the cloth before I put on any resin, pulling it tight to get a good lay.

A newer glassing trick I just saw in North Carolina goes on over bare wood. A mixture of mat fibers and resin is sprayed on the bottom and sides to the waterline with a gun. It seems to work okay and it looks good.

If you plan to do any or all of this, by all means get the Defender Industries catalogue before you start. It has the most comprehensive guide and drawings anywhere.

Fiberglass over Aluminum

Fiberglass will stick to aluminum if the flexing of the boat isn't too severe. If the boat twists and distorts when in use, the glass will crack eventually.

For best adherence use epoxy resin. Grind away any paint and use a coarse sandpaper to impart "tooth" to the metal surface, which will increase adhesion. Some aluminum primers accomplish this. If there is any chance of any oily substance being on the surface, wash the area with acetone before applying the cloth. Lay the cloth in place and saturate it with resin. You don't need the first prime coat since there will be no absorption into the metal. Let the first coat dry, then add a second coat. This should be enough, but if it appears that the cloth is not well saturated, add a third coat. Second and third coats can be polyester.

I once saw an aluminum johnboat in which the L section along the bottom of the seats had pulled loose from the bottom. To regain rigidity and waterproof the holes, the section had been taped with glass. I asked how long the tapes held and was told that it had been several years.

Royalex

Royalex is an extremely tough plastic now used extensively in canoe construction. It can take woeful punishment and still bounce back into shape. In fact, the people at Old Town Canoe Co. got a lot of publicity when they took a bunch of their Royalex canoes to the top of their four-story factory and threw them off! They merely bounced in the parking lot.

While it is tough to damage, it is equally difficult to repair. Some suggested epoxies are available from the following: Uniroyal # DC 2490: Adhesive Dept., Uniroyal Inc., Mishawaka, IN 46544. Ren 1250: Ren Plastics, 5424 S. Cedar Rd., Lansing MI 48910. Thermoset 110: Thermoset Plastics, 5101 55 St., Indianapolis, IN 46226; Epoxical 606: U.S. Gypsum, 101 S. Wacker Dr., Chicago, IL 60611.

Royalex can also be painted with an acrylic air-dry paint. Du Pont is one company that offers acrylic paints.

R. E. Butler, a friend who has aided me in the past, obtained this information from Uniroyal, the manufacturers, and reprinted it in the Float Fishermen of Virginia newsletter.

5

Understanding Design

If you are looking for a boat to customize, you'll meet a bewildering variety of types and designs. To help understand and evaluate them, you should know the general principles of hull design. While the performance of a finished boat is affected by many things, there are inherent characteristics in different designs and even interiors.

Displacement vs. Planing

To begin with, there are two types of boat hulls based on performance characteristics. *Displacement boats* slip easily through the water with minimum push. Their hulls ease the water out of the way and, with little wasted energy, ease it back. Canoes and most sailboats are the best-known displacement types. The less effort required to move (displace) the water, the better. As such, the displacement hull can be propelled with the least amount of energy. A stroke on a canoe paddle shoots the vessel ahead 10 feet or more. A wisp of air can keep a sailboat "ghosting" along. Fashionable now are the so-called "trawler" yachts. A 50-foot displacement vessel will move along at 8 mph and burn no more than a few gallons of fuel an hour.

The disadvantage of a displacement hull is that it has a limited top speed. It can go only so fast. If you try to push it beyond this speed, it will only make the stern squat deeper in the water and the energy will be dissipated in making larger and larger waves. Generally, the longer the waterline length, the faster the boat. But about 10 mph is top speed for the vast majority of displacement yachts.

Planing boats lift out of the water under the push of power or sail and skim on top of the surface. As they go faster and faster, they lift higher and higher, until when running at top speed, the well-designed planing boat leaves very little wake. In its ultimate form — the racing three-point hydroplane — the only parts of the boat actually in the water are the ends of the sponsons and the lower blade of the propeller. Given greater and greater power with no added weight, a planing boat is theoretically capable of unlimited speeds. In practice, however, added power means added weight. And a problem of racing boats is that at high speeds they tend to act like an airplane wing and take off the water, often with disastrous results, since rudder control is lost.

The differences between displacement and planing hulls are not always so clear-cut as this makes it sound. A decade ago, offshore sailboats, light and strong, were going faster than was theoretically possible. The hulls were lifting out of the water slightly and planing.

Weight-carrying aspects of a flat-bottomed johnboat show here. Stern is hardly depressed. (Courtesy Monark Boat Co., Monticello, Ark.)

A flat-bottomed rowboat is a displacement hull when it is rowed. Put power to it and the flatness will drive out of the water on plane. Conversely, planing boats function as displacement boats in their lowest speed ranges. You have all seen planing boats running slowly, leaving little or no wake. The water is slipping past them with little wasted energy.

With the exception of canoes, most small boats used today for hunting or fishing are planing hulls. How do you tell when a boat is on plane? When the entire transom is out of the water.

Flat Bottom vs. Round or V Bottom

The flat bottom is the most basic boat shape. There are so many flat-bottomed boats because it is a superb design. It is the easiest to design and build out of steel, wood, or aluminum. It is the most stable hull known. You can stand on the side of a johnboat with a broad beam and the boat will hardly tip. A flat-bottomed boat will carry its load less deep in the water than any other design because every underwater inch is lifting. Nothing beats the flat bottom for shallow draft. For the same reason, the shape planes more easily than any other. Resistance of water against the broad flat underbody pushes or "lifts" the boat out of its medium. Since every inch of its underbody is lifting surface, it is the fastest and most efficient user of power of all hull designs. Given the same weight and length boat and same horsepower motor, one with a flat bottom will go faster and/or be more economical than other types, all else being equal.

The lazy streams of the Ozarks gave rise to these long johnboats, almost canoelike in length-to-beam relationship. (Courtesy Missouri Conservation Commission; Photo by Don Wooldridge)

The V-bottom hull incorporates sharpness forward where the hull meets the waves but flattens aft to create lift.

As you reduce beam in relation to length, the flattie sinks into the water and becomes more tippy. Yet it remains a superb hull. The deeper draft "grips" the water. Round the edges slightly and point the ends and you have the basic canoe shape. Curiously, the underwater hull shape of a 250,000-ton supertanker is almost exactly the same.

These long, lean flatties push through the water — displace it — and are comfortable in rough water. But pounding is the Waterloo of the broad-beamed flattie. Skimming over the surface, its bottom meets every wave with a tooth-jarring smack.

Sailing people meet this problem by rounding the bottom. So do designers of high-speed planing boats. The more roundness, the softer the ride, but comfort is bought at the price of lift. What designers try to do is build in deep roundness from the bow aft to about midship because this is the area that meets the waves. The section aft that the boat rides on and that stays in the water is flattened out to gain lifting sufaces.

The same principle was applied to V-bottom boats when plywood was introduced and made building round-bottom hulls difficult. Forward where the boat meets the waves there is a deep V. Aft the V all but disappears to put the flattie's lifting abilities to work. When fiberglass took over, designers often combined the two, creating a deep V forward and flattening it out into a round shape aft.

Yet what happens when you drive a boat so fast through rough water that *all* of the boat comes out of the water? Answer: it pounds. If you don't slow down, the boat will pound itself to pieces. In the late 1950s Ray Hunt, a Massachusetts naval architect, created a boat with a severe deep V forward, and he carried the angle of the V un-changed all the way to the transom. The underwater knife blade created a superb rough-water boat but retained enough lift to plane efficiently. Hunt's inspiration was to include flat sections called lifting strakes that run the length of the hull. They don't hamper riding characteristics but make it possible to plane the hull with even greater efficiency. They also act as keels. A word about keels. You can add a keel to any of these hulls. Essentially a keel makes the boat keep on course better at a cost of making it more difficult to move sideways and turn in a tight radius.

Is the deep V the "best" hull form? Not by any means. There are extreme disadvan-tages to the design. The wedge draws a lot of water. A 20-foot, conventional V boat might draw 15 inches; the same boat in deep V draws 25 inches. Single-engine power worsens this aspect because the propeller must be low enough to completely clear the lowest point of the V. And despite the lifting strakes, much horsepower is expended in keeping the boat on plane. But probably the main problem with the deep V is stability at rest: The boats are uncomfortably tippy.

By the 1960s, fiberglass was dominating boatbuilding. Fiberglass can take any shape. Ray Hunt and Dick Cole, a Miami architect, came up with similar ideas. They kept the deep V for riding comfort but added little Vs (called sponsons) on either side for stability at rest. We see this design today in endless variations; some forms carry the V aft, others flatten the stern section to gain lift. Usually the forward Vs extend from a third to two thirds down the hull length. The longer they are, the greater the stability, but the rougher the boat rides — that is, the more it pounds — in a head sea. The first two boats made to this design were the Boston Whaler and the Thunderbird. Both were instant

Ocean racers are out of the water as much as in it. You can imagine these razor-V hulls leaping from sea crest to sea crest in rough ocean races.

successes and sell briskly under a host of names—trihedral, cathedral, air slot, gull-wing. These boats "track" beautifully. That is, they stay on course and slide like a porpoise down following seas. They are superstable, carry a huge load comparable to the flatties, and are equally shoal draft. Forward the bow is usually blunted to add the full width of the hull to the forward section. Because air is trapped and partially compressed under the hull at high speeds, claims are made for a "cushioned" ride. This is probably somewhat true at high speeds in smaller seas, but when the big seas roll any cushioning quickly disappears.

Suppose you took the sharp V of the deep V and chopped off some of the tip, making the end of it a flat, lifting surface. Would that work? If you retained maximum V, you could add sponsons. Or if you chop the V back severely, maybe you wouldn't need the sponsons. What about dropping the boat deeper in the water? You could beef up the chines. Would they then add to stability? Would any or all of this work? You bet. This is the area of the so-called modified V. The variations on the V are endless, and designers will undoubtedly experiment with them forever. The latest "hot" designs are the so-called "pad" bass boats in which the end of the deep V smooths out into a flat section. At lower speeds the V works to soften the ride, yet when the boat's speed increases it finally lifts up and runs only on the pad. This reduces the wetted surface, which in turn lessens friction with the water—that is, drag.

Console vs. No Console

It is vital to know what the underwater design of your vessel is intended to do. But the boat buyer and customizer these days is faced with equally difficult choices based on how the boat is laid out. There are two basic interiors. What I'll call *conventional*, because it is older, is a boat with a small forward deck, behind which is a windshield and helmsman's seat, usually on the right side (because any boat approaching from the right has the right of way), and an open cockpit extending the rest of the way aft. Some boats leave off the deck, thus opening the forward section, and call themselves bow riders.

The newer basic layout is the *console* boat. Console boats are completely open and mount the controls on a box (console) in the middle of the boat. The helmsman's seat is behind the console.

Dick Fisher, who founded the famed Boston Whaler company, told me he invented the console. He had spent the winter building the plug for the 17-footer (the little 13-footer came first). In April he put it overboard for testing. Since it was a test for hull performance only, the interior was left completely stripped. Fisher planned to power the boat with a 75-hp Johnson outboard motor, but there was no place to mount the controls. To facilitate things, a big box was built and mounted in the center of the boat. During the testing, Fisher had what he called "several knowledgeable types" aboard. All agreed that standing up to run a small boat was dashing, manly, and comfortable. The canny Fisher took due note and designed the immensely successful mahogany console that took Whaler's name to the front rank.

Coburn and Sargeant brought out this version of the Keys tarpon and bonefish skiffs. The boat's clean lines and open design were an instant success. AquaSport and Mako soon fielded versions of their own.

Like everything else about boats, there are some things to be said for both designs. Because they are so fundamental and different, let's look at both.

Without doubt the single great advantage of a center-station steering console in the middle of a boat is that it allows you to conn the vessel standing up. You can see so much more. How many times do fish reveal themselves visually? A swirl or an odd surface movement shows or you see a discoloration of the water caused by baitfish or gamefish schools. Birds over bait are a clear signal. If you're standing up, with full 360-degree visibility, you're going to spot more fish signs than the guy seated behind a windshield. To get a dramatic demonstration of this, climb the flying bridge of the next big sportfisherman you get a chance to visit. It's like opening a door. The whole watery world opens to you for miles when moments ago, down on the deck, your vision was restricted to a few hundred yards. And the fact that instead of looking across the water you're looking down into it makes telltale fish signs even easier to spot.

Increased visibility helps in other ways. You can handle the boat better since you're sitting in the middle of it, seeing all of it. If you want to hold in a certain position to cast to a shoreline or rock pile, for example, a standing position amidships can't be beat.

Conning a boat from a standing position offers the advantage of allowing the shock of bouncing through the waves to be partially absorbed by your legs. If you bend your knees slightly, hard bumps tend to disappear. A tip that console skippers might pick up from ocean racers is to lay a piece of ½-inch foam rubber on the deck where you stand and cover it with a piece of ⅜-inch or ½-inch plywood. It's astonishing how much shock the foam will absorb.

In addition to the physical advantages of conning your boat from a center console is the psychological factor. It can be very invigorating and refreshing to feel the wind and spray in your face. In my opinion it is this factor, more than any other, that has caused the great popularity of the console.

Another advantage of a console is that it opens the boat beautifully for casting. Here the design cannot be faulted. The wide-open boat, with the forward portion undecked (and often with a raised casting platform), allows three lead-slingers to operate at once. If you do much target casting and your boat has a windshield, you've probably worked out some arrangement where you sit on the back of the helmsman's seat to cast. Or you stand up next to the wheel and lean over from time to time to handle the boat. Casting can be done, but not nearly so comfortably. If it's rough, the console or the seat behind it offer a ready bracing platform. Wedged against either you can keep both hands free to work the rod.

Insofar as exposure to the elements is concerned, the console arrangement leaves much to be desired. While there are certainly times when it is fun to be in the open air and sun, the times can be few in a lot of places. How many days a year do you run with convertible top down in Milwaukee, where it's usually too cold, or Biloxi, where the sun is usually too hot?

The console of the superstar Boston Whaler leaves both ends of the boat open for casting. For visibility and casting, a console boat can't be beat.

And while most consoles have windshields, they are puny compared with the huge hunk of glass found on conventional boats. In a console boat, you are pretty much at the mercy of the blast. This is okay at low speeds, but in today's 30-mph-plus boats if you find yourself in the uncomfortable position of having to come home against a fresh breeze, you're being blasted by a 40- to 60-mile wind. If you have to run very far, like several hours, believe me, the romance drains away quickly.

The same is true of spray. I've watched fishermen come home in console boats on nice sunny but windy days dressed in full foul-weather suits. The spray was hosing them down, and they had no place to hide.

Now you're going to tell me that with today's folding canvas tops and plastic curtains a console can be closed in just like the top of a windshield-equipped boat. This is true to a certain extent. The folding top is okay because tough aluminum frames and nylon guys can hold it. And by itself it doesn't present enough wind resistance to pull out the fastenings that hold it. Start putting sidecurtains and clear plastic screens across the front and you start having problems trying to keep them from tearing apart. The best are the turtle-shell covers that enclose the entire bow section because they can be seated to in-deck fasteners around front and sides.

Now we'll take a look at the conventional, or windshield-equipped, boat — which is not passé by any means. In the 1950s when gearshift outboard motors achieved sufficient horsepower to push boats in the 15- to 18-foot range, someone invented simple, inexpensive remote controls for them. This enabled manufacturers for the first time to build outboards in the traditional runabout configuration that conventionally powered inboard boats had enjoyed for years. It was, and is, an eminently successful interior layout. A forward deck extends a quarter or a third of the way aft. Where it stops, a windshield stands. This can either be a wraparound or come with various tricky opening devices that seal off, not only the front of the boat, but the sides as well. Thick plastic or glass built into strongly supported aluminum frames makes most windshields strong enough to use as a handhold. The helm seat is on the right. A companion stands against the opposite rail with a narrow but adequate walkway between.

Hard wooden seats were replaced by foldout back-to-back seats, often with ingenious storage space underneath. Foam rubber and rhino-hided plastics make them tough, easy to clean, and comfortable. The foldout element allows them to be used as bunks, and the back-to-back feature faces the sitter toward the stern, perfect for trolling.

For many years this was the standard cockpit arrangement. It is still by far the most common for a variety of reasons. The first might be called versatile comfort. You can be comfortable in the boat under a wide range of conditions.

Since the windshield figures in this, let's explain that first. The strength of it absorbs the wind blast, yet its top edge can be drilled to take strong fastenings to which a canvas top can be attached. In some versions, the top folds up on the top of the windshield. On others it goes all the way down to store neatly out of the way on the forward deck.

The braces for the windshield extend back on either side of the driver's and companion seats. These too are strong places to fasten plastic curtains. Even the whole back opening of the boat from top to floor can be closed in with a curtain. Since this meets no wind resistance, it tends to last a long time and presents few problems.

Do you see now the many options you have with this rig? If it's hot sun, put up the top, open the windshield. Beautiful sunny day—open everything up and sit on the back of the seat. Stormy—rain or spray—button up. All hands stay warm and dry with side and top protection. Is it cold but the cohos are still biting? Close everything up. If it's important cold, add a catalytic heater between the seats.

The forward deck has both negative and positive aspects. It absorbs a generous amount of interior space. Often it makes it hard to tie the boat up. (On many small boats you have to practically risk your neck just to get forward.) On the plus side, it provides a handy, dry storage area for wet-weather gear, radio, tackle, etc. On most of the boats I see, everything usually gets thrown in a gigantic pile (does anybody remember Fibber McGee's closet?), but you can install hooks, lockers, shock cord–protected shelves, and so on to fully utilize the space if driven by unreasonable ambition.

Open windshield allows the breeze to keep this boat cool, but the windshield takes the spray when running in rough water. Cuddy under deck offers dry storage.

The deck makes the vessel a tiny bit safer, because it prevents taking a sea over the bow. This seldom happens because of the self-protective nature of boats. By the time conditions reach that point, most skippers have long ago retreated.

There is more pounding in the forward position. It is an undeniable fact that the farther aft you go in a boat the smoother the ride is.

Certainly the windshield impairs visibility. When the spray is flying, it's often hard to see other boats, much less fish.

To close the discussion somewhat abruptly, there aren't many other differences between the two versions, no matter what you may be told. The hull form is the same whatever the interior. Correct balance depends on weight location and motor drive angle, and either version allows variation of these. The deck adds strength, but plastic boats are so strong that the difference is meaningless. Flotation can be added to either hull. The cost of console vs. deck-windshield is a standoff; one is as bad as the other. Gas cans go neatly out of the way under most consoles, but it is a nuisance dragging them in and out. Under the motor well aft is certainly an acceptable stowage spot.

6
Understanding Boat Construction

Since you don't want to be limited in the boats you can dredge up and rehabilitate for your special hunting and fishing needs, you should have some general idea of the various kinds of construction. There are all kinds and many are complex, but you must not lose heart. It is a new language coming at you in large quantities. But you don't have to know the names of the pieces to figure out that this piece here fastens to that piece there.

General Wood Construction

Wood boats are built from a skeleton. The keel is the backbone. In small boats it is laid on horses or, if it's curved, in a long mold cut to shape that will be discarded later. Since it's easy to turn small boats over, they are usually built upright for the skeleton, turned over for planking, and righted again for the interiors.

With the keel in position, at the front end is attached a piece (stem) that forms the bow. At the back is a flat section called a *transom*. To add strength, a knee distributes the thrust of a motor high on the transom to the keel. With a head and tail attached, we add ribs, properly called *frames*. These are fastened to the keel at intervals and will receive the bottom and side planking. These frames really shape the boat. Where the side and bottom planks join in a V-bottomed or flat-bottomed boat, there isn't enough material in the planking alone to create a watertight joint, so a long member on each side of the boat is fitted into each frame and fastened to the stem and transom. These two members are called *chines*, and because the angle of the facing areas changes as the chines curve the length of the boat, fitting them requires the most skill of all. So that water in the boat can run freely to the lowest point to be bailed out, holes called *limber holes* are cut into the bottom of the frames.

This skeleton provides the inherent strength of a boat. If the wood is strong—*sound* is the boatbuilding term—and the fastenings are not corroded, the boat is sound even

33

though it may be extremely old. If the skeleton is weak, no amount of patching, caulking, or fiberglassing will last for long. And since all these parts are carefully fitted together, it's woefully difficult to take any one out and repair it. Too many other parts are affected or busted up in the taking-out process. So if you're looking over a boat, check the skeleton first. And don't be afraid to draw out screws, bolts, or nails to see if they are unaffected by corrosion.

Now you are ready to plank. If you plank longitudinally, the planks next to the keel are called *garboards*. You'll hear about them because they are the the first to loosen up and start to leak. The bottom planking overlaps the sides. If you plank with cedar, some small space must be left between to allow the wood to swell. Most amateurs like to use plywood because the angles are less curvy and it is easy to work. Usually plywood is nailed and glued; the nails in effect hold the members in place while the glue sets up. To take a plywood boat apart, usually you must chisel the pieces apart. This usually wrecks the plywood planking and often the chine as well. It tears up your chisel too as you hit the nails with it.

Sweet lines of a Jersey skiff are typical of lapstrake construction. Hull is planked and limber oak frames are steamed and "walked" in place and riveted.

At this point turn the boat upright. The sides will go in and out like an accordion, so you need bracing. The first brace is the *gunwale*, pronounced and often spelled *gunnel*. The gunwale goes on the outside of the hull at the top of the side. Often to help stiffen a boat, a piece called an *inwale* is fastened to the inside top of the frames. At the point on the deck where the sides meet the transom, usually two additional horizontal knees distribute the motor's thrust to the planking and frames.

If you are decking the boat, the tops of the frames must be notched to receive another chine. Then curved pieces to support the deck, called *carlings*, fasten into this and the tops of frames. These can be easily sawed to shape, but doing so requires a hellacious amount of material. On several occasions, I've built carlings out of plywood laminations. Before you saw, check that the plywood is cut on the bendy side. Position your frames so a frame forms the forward and aft end of your cockpit. For the cockpit sides, fit in a straight coaming piece that sticks up enough so you can put a hatch on it. The coaming also prevents water from running into the boat. Attach a similar curved coaming to the fore and aft frames. Between the coaming and the side, you'll probably need two or more half-carlings that fasten on one end to frame tops and on the other to the coaming.

That's all there is to a boat.

Round Hulls

The traditional round hull so often found in sailboats is occasionally found in smaller outboard or inboard boats. They are usually too tricky for us amateurs to build. The frames must be elaborately sawed and usually fitted and laminated. Or they are steamed in a big long box, bent over forms, and clamped there to take the proper curves. Too tough! And all the curving surfaces require exacting skill to make joints correct and tight. However, if you find a sound hull built this way that suits you, such boats are not too difficult to modify by adding or removing decks and so forth.

Lapstraked Hulls

Strake is another word for *plank*. Let's say you want to strengthen the boat by fastening the planks to one another. Lay or lap each plank over the one below it just enough to take a fastening. You've got a lapstraked boat, also called *clinker-built*. It is a method of construction that is light, strong, and ancient. Viking ships were built this way. So were thousands of Thompson and Penn Yan skiffs in the 1940s and 1950s; many are still in service.

Lapstraked boats are built a little differently. Stem, keel, and transom are laid. Then the planks are curved around forms, each fastened to the next, often with copper rivets, sometimes with bolts and screws. Only after the boat is planked do the frames go in. These are usually green — that is, unkilned — white oak. They are steamed and tamped in place by standing on them; then they are fastened to the planks.

A disadvantage of this method of construction is that the planks can't be caulked well. Never caulk against the fastenings. If you try to push adhesive seam sealers between the lapped planks, the flexing of the planking will soon throw it out. About the only way to stop a lapstraked boat from leaking is to refasten it. This can probably be done only once. After that there won't be enough space on the small area of overlap for another fastener. Another disadvantage with lapstraked wood boats is that they are extremely difficult to repair. You can patch small holes in planking, but taking a shattered plank out and replacing it requires an expert.

Lapstraked boats helped give fiberglass over wood the bad reputation it deserves. Almost all lapstraked boats that have been used at all will leak, so it was natural for owners to try to fiberglass them. Two things were wrong with the idea. First, these light but strong boats flex more than any other boat, which helped loosen the glass. The main problem, though, was that fiberglass is difficult to get into sharp crevices. The harsh angles of the laps allowed the glass to pull away, and initial adhesion was never good. If you do ever want to glass a lapstraked vessel, fill the cracks with fiberglass putty, with quarter-round molding, or, better still, a combination of the two.

Flat-Bottomed Hulls

Flat-bottomed boats are the easiest of all to build. Many a johnboat has come out of the Ozark hills without even a chine. The bottom planks are nailed right to the side planks. Terrible construction, but it apparently works. If the bottom is planked fore and aft, the boat is usually called a *dory* because the Grand Banks dories are built this way. Most flat-bottomed boats are planked athwartship; the planks are nailed to the chines, and an external keel is added later. It's easy to replace or repair planks in any flat-bottomed vessel.

Strip-Planked Hulls

Occasionally you'll see a strip-planked boat. In this method, long, narrow planks are nailed on top of one another and glued to build up the planking. Such a hull can be built around a form and the skeletal members added later. The boats are relatively easy to repair because you cut out a section of the planking and fit new pieces into the void.

Canoe Construction

Canoes and some older prams and outboards are quite capable of being put into hunting and fishing service. These boats are built somewhat like lapstraked vessels. A very light skin usually of cedar planking is built over a form. Then extremely narrow strips of wood, usually ash or birch, are pressed in to serve as frames. The key in this building is in the method of fastening. Since both wood members are so light and thin, there isn't enough inherent holding power in them. Most canoes are clench-nailed, using copper tacks. Clenching, like riveting, is a two-person operation. One person drives the tack all the way through both planking and frame. As the point protrudes, a backing plate is held against the point. This turns the point back on itself in a U so the point reenters the frame. The tack is then driven the rest of the way. The outside planking is held firm by the broad head of the tack, the other side by the area of the clench. The tack cannot work its way free because of the U shape.

I once restored a canoe-built outboard pram I found and liked because of its lines and ultralight construction. After I ripped the canvas off, I used a saber saw and cut the side down to achieve a low profile. I turned the boat on its side and, with my wife's help, refastened the entire boat.

I built in a chine piece where I had cut the hull, added a deck of ¼-inch plywood and a cockpit, and beefed up the outboard bracket with knees to keel and chine.

I gave the entire boat a coat of polyester resin, and the old cedar hull really soaked it up. Then I glassed the bottom with 10-ounce cloth and the deck seams with 3-inch tape.

Older canoes can often be bought for low prices. They build up years of paint, which eventually cracks the canvas. Strip it off, refasten if necessary, and glass with Xynole-polyester or very light cloth. Recanvasing one of these canoes with canvas is an arduous job that calls for a lot of skill. Fiberglass, however, makes it a snap. The final product is watertight and usable in ice, and any added weight is negligible.

7
How to Build a Boat

Everyone is intimidated at the thought of building a boat from scratch. First of all, the building plans are incomprehensible. To build a boat from plans you are forced to learn two whole new skills, each of which amounts to a profession in itself. You must learn what is, in effect, a whole new language. And you must learn to be a draftsman. To this, add a third skill, that of being, if not a master, at least handy, with tools.

Every part of a boat has a name. And you couldn't go take a course in boatbuilding terms if you wanted to. It's strictly learn-it-yourself. But you can get by with a bare handful of essential terms. Why? Because when you are confronted with the actual problem, not words on paper but pieces that must be fitted together, you can see that piece A has to be fitted to piece B and there are only a few ways in which they can be fastened together. Then you'll realize that if the joint isn't to leak you'd better back the joint with piece C.

Boat plans, like boatbuilding language, look tougher than they are. To start with they are frequently drawn on top of one another to save space on a printed page. You look at the boat lines from the bow on and halfway through you are suddenly looking at it from the stern. It's tricky. Don't despair. In the old days of boating when every backyard in coastal towns sported professional builders, most of them couldn't read plans. They built by eye. They knew what the finished boat should look like and just put it together without any fuss. You can too.

Add another factor — what I call the tyranny of construction. There are lots of different ways to build the same boat. A set of plans is one man's idea of how it should be done. You may not want to do it his way, but your way. There is no law that says you have to be a slave to a set of plans.

Really, all you need to build a boat is to be able to measure correctly. There is a thing called a *table of offsets* that shows the exact measurements at various distances (stations) along the hull. Draw these on pieces of paper and the shape of the hull appears before your eyes. Boatbuilders call this *lofting*.

38

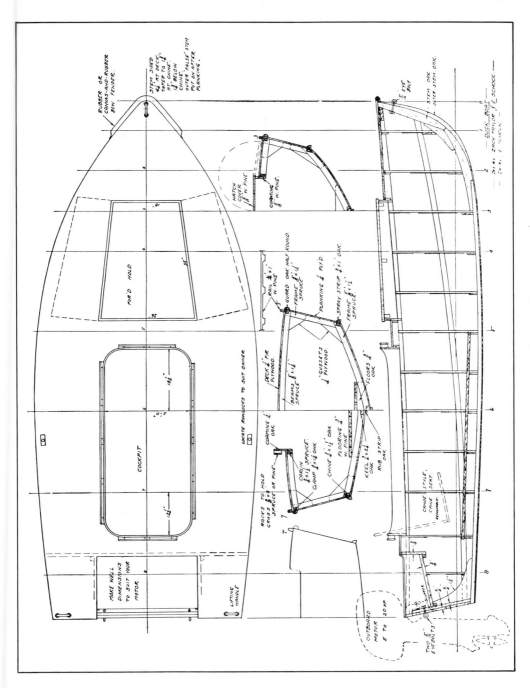

THE ZACKBOX

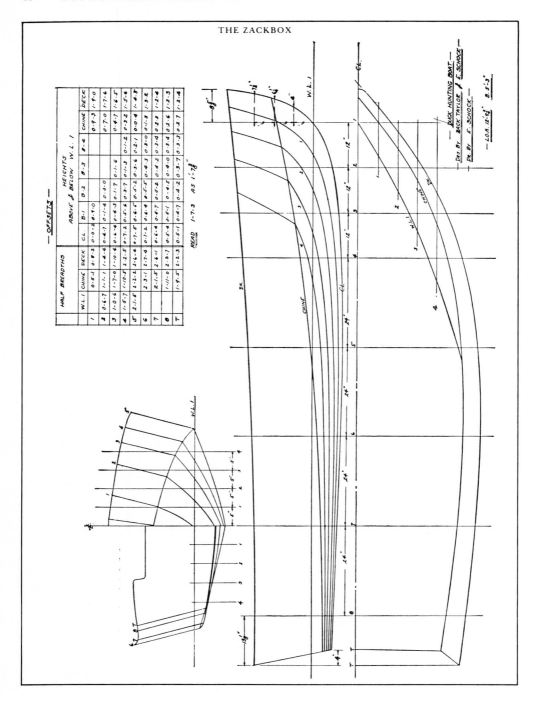

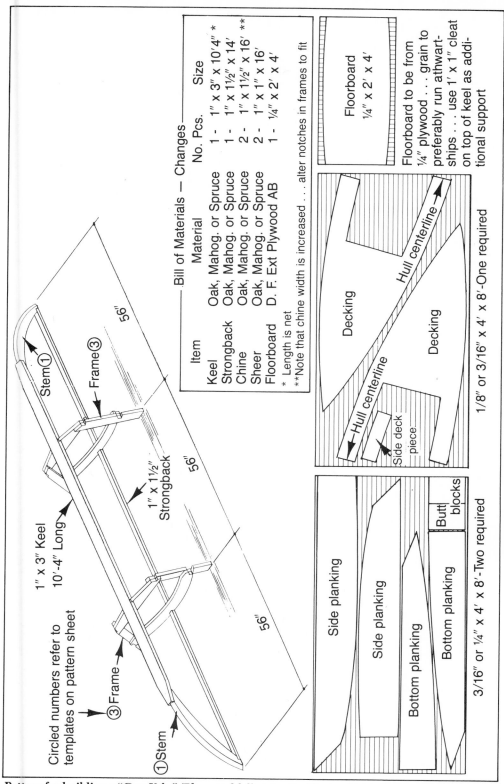

Bill of Materials — Changes

Item	Material	No. Pcs.	Size
Keel	Oak, Mahog. or Spruce	1 -	1" x 3" x 10'4" *
Strongback	Oak, Mahog. or Spruce	1 -	1" x 1½" x 14'
Chine	Oak, Mahog. or Spruce	2 -	1" x 1½" x 16' **
Sheer	Oak, Mahog. or Spruce	2 -	1" x 1" x 16'
Floorboard	D. F. Ext Plywood AB	1 -	¼" x 2' x 4'

* Length is net
**Note that chine width is increased . . . alter notches in frames to fit

Floorboard to be from ¼" plywood . . . grain to preferably run athwartships . . . use 1' x 1" cleat on top of keel as additional support

Floorboard ¼" x 2' x 4'

Decking

Hull centerline

Decking

Hull centerline

Side deck piece

1/8" or 3/16" x 4' x 8'-One required

Side planking

Side planking

Bottom planking

Bottom planking

Butt blocks

3/16" or ¼" x 4' x 8'-Two required

Stem①

Frame③

56"

56"

1" x 1½" Strongback

56"

1" x 3" Keel
10'-4" Long

Circled numbers refer to templates on pattern sheet

③ Frame

①Stem

Pattern for building a "Can-Yak." (Plans and following ten illustrations courtesy Glen L. Marine Designs, 9152 E. Rosecrans, Bellflower, Ca., 90706)

After you set up strongback, add chine pieces at chine and deck.

With a wood rasp and file, shape chines to the angle on which the planking will lie. Use a straightedge to get a neat fit.

Take paper template that you've lofted or bought and lay it against frames to check fit. If it's okay, make a rough cut of planking.

Use clamps to hold planking in place for final fitting. Rasp chines for watertight joint.

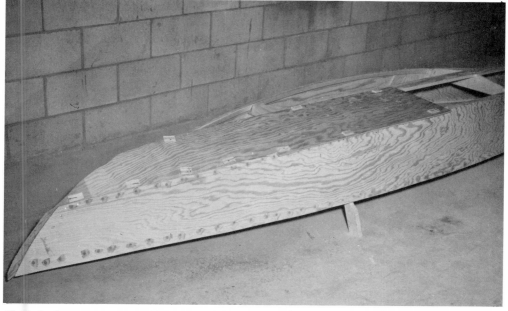

Hull planking goes on. Small blocks prevent screw heads from pulling through plywood as the plank is screwed into place.

Turn the hull over. Fit in the butt blocks on the bottom and the sides. Knees will be used to support the side deck.

Center piece will support the decking. Reinforcing adds to stiffness.

Cut the deck pieces first in rough cut after checking paper templates with actual hull.

The floorboard goes in. It is supported by small blocks.

You've gone this far—might as well make up a paddle.

Also, the boats we'll be talking about in the pages ahead simply aren't all that complicated. In the first place, you'll probably be building in plywood. Any other kind of wood technique may be too complicated. But plywood with its straight lines makes for easy building. And now we have plastic. Wonderful, forgiving plastic. I've built maybe a half-dozen duckboats and none leaked a drop, even though I couldn't make a watertight joint to save my life. You merely round the joint slightly and glass on a piece of fiberglass tape. Watertight forever. Drill a hole in the wrong place? Slap in the fiberglass putty and press on regardless.

The same principle applies if you are building in fiberglass. If you want to build a duplicate of a Wellcraft overnighter, you need a factory and a resident genius. Building a duckboat using super-simple techniques is another matter.

Books for Boatbuilders

There are grand books that anyone even slightly interested in small boats and building should have. Two are by Howard I. Chapelle. First is *American Small Sailing Craft* (1951, W. W. Norton & Co.). This is a magnificent classic. Chapelle has listed and catalogues virtually all the early vessels in this country's colorful marine history. Among them are many fine fishermen and several plans for duckboats, including the traditional Barnegat sneakbox. The other is *Boatbuilding* (1941, W. W. Norton & Co.). Despite its age this is the definitive work on the subject. Chapelle's plans and instructions are concise and clear, and his sparkling personality eases the burden of learning all the terminology. I've always loved his theory that every boatbuilder's shop should contain a "groaning chair." After a bad mistake you can sit in the chair and groan about it. A friend of mine bought this book twenty years ago, and when I saw it I instantly and blatantly stole it from him. I've spent hours and hours not just reading it but studying it. Chapelle's drawings are a delight and make me green with envy.

Boatbuilding should be considered for traditional building methods. There are newer aids. *Boat Building with Plywood* (1962) is by Glenn L. Witt, one of the boat kit manufacturers. *Boatbuilding & Repairing in Fiberglass* (1972), by Melville Willis, is good for plastic builders. Add *How to Build a Fiberglass Boat* (1975), by Klaus Voss. All the above can be ordered by contacting International Marine Publishing, Camden, ME 04843.

Shortcut Construction

The easiest way to build a boat is to let someone else do it for you. If you can find a fiberglass hull that you like, you can probably buy it in shell form from the manufacturer. This is a common practice among the sailboat set. With the hull assembly and maybe the deck too, you can customize the interior to your heart's desire knowing that the design is good and the essentials are sound.

If you want to build in wood, you'll be wise to spend $3 or so and order catalogues from the several fine firms that sell boat kits and find a hull there that suits you. Once you've built a correct, sound hull, you can modify and customize.

There are a number of good reasons for going the kit route. First, the plans and building instructions are detailed and aimed at amateurs. There isn't the complicated jargon. And all the kit manufacturers have received so much feedback on their plans that they've long since worked and reworked the areas that amateurs have difficulty understanding.

Second, in addition to the plans, the kit makers offer patterns or templates. As mentioned, these are just like dress patterns. They are full-scale paper cutouts of the pieces of the boat. If you want a transom, spread out the transom template and draw the outline on the proper piece of wood. Then cut on these lines. We'll discuss how to make these patterns yourself by reading off the measurements from the table of offsets. But it's much easier when somebody else has done the demanding task for you. Plans and patterns run from $20 for a small boat to $150 for a 35-footer or so.

Third, the kit manufacturers offer frame kits of their models. The essential components are precut for you. Say you want to put a complicated bevel edge in a stem. It will take you hours to measure and fit it properly. A kit manufacturer can set up his woodworking machine and turn out a hundred in an hour, each exactly right. These frame kits are the skeleton of the vessel, and because machine tools can make them so easily they add little to the cost beyond the cost of the wood. A typical frame kit for a 15-footer plus plans and patterns will cost about $150.

A last good reason for the kit approach is that they offer good buys on fastenings, hardware, and even fiberglass. Most of the kit boats are plywood, but some have gone to fiberglass.

Look for new manufacturers that advertise usually in the classified pages of the outdoor and home-builder magazines. The ones I know are: Glen L. Marine Designs, 9152 E. Rosecrans, Bellflower, CA 90706, catalogue $1; Clarkcraft, 16-X Aqualane, Tonawanda, NY 14150, catalogue $2; and Luger Industries, 3800 West Highway, Burnsville, MN 55378.

Lofting

Lofting is the boatbuilding term for making your own patterns from the measurements given in the table of offsets that accompany every plan. There are a lot of good reasons to loft any boat before building it. It catches any errors in the measurements. And instead of a little box of hen scratches, you have the whole boat laid out before your eyes. Another advantage of lofting is that when you draw you are also subconsciously building the boat too.

To start, go to a lumberyard and buy about 45 feet of builder's construction paper. You'll need a piece several feet longer than the boat you'll build. Scotch-tape or tack this piece to the floor. First draw the boat in full scale sideways. Draw a straight line longer than your boat. You may have to use a chalk line for this, or the side of a plywood panel. This is your baseline. Now go to the table of offsets and measure off the "height above baseline" for each of the "stations," that is, positions usually where the frames are. When you have them all out, use a light bendy piece of wood to draw the sheer line. (The sheer is the curve in the top of the hull.) Now draw the boat looking down on it. Since both sides of a boat are supposed to be the same, only half the measurements are given from your centerline. You can use the same centerline or strike a new one. In the "half-breadths" section you'll find the measurements. Draw these out on both sides. Then draw the frames. The table of offsets shows the head-on profile for the bow half of the boat and stern-to profile for the after section. Measure these and draw them in full scale. When you go about the actual building, you'll take all the measurements from these full-size plans.

Actually lofting is a complicated procedure. I've oversimplified it here. Frankly, I've always taken my own advice and used existing hulls that I've modified. If you get serious about a boat design you can acquire no other way than building from plans, you'll certainly want a book specifically on lofting. A good one is *Boat Building with Plywood* by Gene Witt, 9152 Rosecrans, Bellflower, CA 90706, $8.95.

Tools

Anyone would be crazy to build or customize a boat without power tools. You'll need a ¼-inch drill — a ⅜-inch is better — with appropriate-sized metal and wood bits. If you are going to be fiberglassing, get a disc-sander attachment. And if you plan to work a lot in fiberglass, a ⅜-inch or ½-inch drill with disc has the power to really make the resin fly. You can also use a belt or disc sander. A saber saw is more versatile than a circular saw. You can cut holes and round corners with the saber. But a circular saw cuts a straighter edge unless you aid the saber with a guide strip. Again, if you start with a ⅜-inch or larger drill you can get a circular attachment. But a circular or bench saw is better.

You'll need a handsaw for careful work. A good backsaw with a miter box is helpful. A good adjustable-cut plane will come in handy, and if you have it professionally sharpened, it will serve you better. I wouldn't be without my automatic screwdrivers, but you'll need assorted sizes of screwdrivers. Add a couple of pairs of pliers with wire cutters. A claw hammer with a standard 16-ounce head is okay, and a tack hammer is a must if you're working in light stuff. You'll need a mill file about 10 inches long and a rattail about 8 inches long for opening holes. Always buy the best files you can because the cheap ones don't stand up. I find a wood rasp a handy item to round edges or rough away my mistakes.

Clamps are important in boatbuilding. So far I've gotten by with two with a 5-inch spread and two with about a 3-inch spread. I use heavy-duty shock cord at times to hold glued pieces tightly together.

Good measuring tools are a must. I have a couple of squares, one about 6 inches with a level in the head and another about 18 inches. I finally broke down and bought an aluminum yardstick and don't know how I lived so long without it. A tape measure will come in handy.

You probably have just about everything I've mentioned, because if you're interested in building a boat you've probably built other things — kitchen cabinets or whatever — and have accumulated both tools and skill. But if you do need to buy tools for your boat project, don't just get the cheapest. A circular saw from the middle of a manufacturer's line may be only $15 more but incomparably better than the saw at the bottom of the line.

Building in Fiberglass

It's easier to build a boat out of fiberglass than most people realize. Before I attempted such a project, however, I'd seek outside help beyond the confines of these pages. There are excellent books available: *How to Fiberglass Boats* by Glen L. Witt, 9152 Rosecrans, Bellflower, CA 90706, $5.95; *Airex-Fiberglass Sandwich Construction*, Thomas Johannson, International Marine, Camden, ME 04843, $8.95; *C-Flex*, Seemann Plastics, P. O. Box 13704, New Orleans, LA 70185, price on request. These books will teach you plenty about techniques. You might also seek personal advice. Any boatyard today has fiberglass experts who can help you. And plastic is such common stuff that your local newspaper can probably put you in contact with someone who works with the stuff all the time.

However, since to customize an existing fiberglass boat you should have some kind of knowledge of how a glass boat is built from scratch, we can generalize on the subject here.

Building from a Shell

The first suggestion about building in glass is: Don't. As in all other kinds of boat-building, don't build unless it is absolutely the only way to get the boat you want. Most fiberglass-boat manufacturers will sell you the boat parts just as they come out of the mold. You join them together and finish any interior. This works somewhat better with sailboats because sailboats don't need the internal stiffening members that powerboats do. The bulkheads and keel usually give sailing vessels, with their lower stresses, enough strength.

For a small powerboat you should purchase the hull and deck and join the two with tape. Kit fiberglass canoes come in several hull sections that fit together for lower shipping costs. You tape the sections together. Tape on a keel, add gunwales, and fit in seats. Larger powerboats have a hull molded in one section. Long braces fore and aft connect to the transom and transfer stresses throughout the hull. In the case of an inboard-outboard or conventional engine, these members are the "beds" that the motors are bolted into. These are usually fiberglass-covered plywood, or in some boats plastic grids. Then an inner liner sits in the hull. This is the cockpit floor on which you stand. It is attached to the hull. In the trade they say it is "welded" to the hull. This simply means that it is glued in place with plastic or maybe capped in some areas with a mat or cloth tape. The deck is welded to the top sections of the inner liner and/or hull. It should be welded, but some builders use self-tapping screws for this.

Copying an Existing Boat

Because of the shortage of builders making duckboats out of *any* material, it's probable you won't be able to find a builder from whom you can buy completed sections to join them yourself. Yet here's a pal that has a duckboat that's exactly what you want. To have one for your own puts you in the boatbuilding business.

The proper way to build a fiberglass boat, at least the way 90 percent of them are built, is in a female mold. You sand a wood copy of hull or deck, called a *plug*, as fine as you can because any imperfections will be transferred on. Then the plug is treated with mold release, and glass mat and cloth are laid up in several layers over it. This is reinforced externally to prevent distortion and broken away from the plug. This is the female mold, and it is further sanded and smoothed and used as a mold for subsequent boats. Similar molds are struck for the hull, inner liner, and deck.

This method is okay if you have a few buddies who all want the same boat. However, for only one boat, it's costly because the mold isn't good for anything after the boat you want is built.

The crudest way to beat the system is to use the existing boat as the plug and lay fiberglass over it. This will be the finished hull. I say crudest because it is very difficult to get a smooth finish to the external glass. And the exterior of most boats, especially duckboats, isn't all that smooth to begin with. A great deal of grinding, filing, and sanding will be in order. But since the ducks will never comment on your handiwork, let's proceed.

First, take the hull and turn it over. Remember, if it is painted, polyester will pull the paint off. This won't affect the strength of the glass much, but the flecks will remain in it, and, of course, the boat will need repainting.

Now you need an agent so you will be able to break the bond between the glass and the boat. Fiberglass will not stick to cellophane. You can spread cellophane over the hull's bottom, tacking it down if necessary or gluing it to a glass hull. Another way to do this is to use a wax, called mold release agent, that prevents adhesion. Defender sells it for $4.95 a quart. The mold release is painted on the hull. It is this stuff, incidentally, that must be washed off a new fiberglass boat hull before bottom paint will stick to it.

Lay a layer of cloth over the hull as smoothly as it will go on and saturate it with resin. Try to make it as smooth as possible. When this dries, add another layer until you build up to the required strength. When you're satisfied that the hull will be strong enough, lift the hull and turn the boat over. Now repeat the procedure with the deck. I think I'd back this with PVC foam and add an inner skin as described later.

How many layers of cloth you need to make the boat strong enough is a hard question to answer from this far away from your boat. There are so many ways to achieve strength. If you have several bulkheads, for example, you don't need as much strength in the hull and/or deck panels. Ribs and cross-bracing add strength. If you're copying an existing fiberglass boat, try to build it the same as the original, copying type and size of materials.

You now have two separate pieces. Grind or saw the ragged edges until they fit as tightly as possible. Now tape the two together. If you want beauty, you must get inside the hull and apply the tape inside. If you just want the strength, you can tape over the outside edges and feather the edges after the tape dries. You have a boat.

Of course, there is a lot more to it than that. If you are going to use an outboard, you might want to glass in a plywood transom. Or bolt on a piece of plywood. And you have to add hardware. Use bolts throughout. The law now requires that you add foam flotation. And you may want to fix in wooden thwarts or even mold your own seats. If substantial power is to be used, the hull must be braced. Usually this is done with plywood stringers taped into the hull. Use ½-inch waterproof plywood in 3-inch strips and lay one down the keel and outside stringers between it and the chine. Completely enclose the plywood in glass cloth, bonding it to the bottom and transom. Cut limber holes so water can drain into the lowest hull position. Add the foam after the stringers are in place.

Core Materials: Airex PVC and C-Flex

Both C-Flex and Airex PVC are core materials that handle easy, are dry, and are extremely flexible. In using them you build the simplest possible mold in the shape of the hull or deck that you want. Then the core is tacked, screwed, or tied with string in position on the mold. When the hull is fair and proper, resin is applied. The core material absorbs this and dries in hardened form. At this point it is broken off the mold and a fiberglass skin is applied first to the outside and then to the inside. In effect you have two hulls, decks or transoms joined to one rigid flotation block. If the boat is to be powered, a series of internal stringers or bracings should be added.

Building a simple small duckboat, I would attempt to use a pal's vessel as the mold. The problem is getting the C-Flex or PVC to lie smoothly in place. After applying mold release you can try tacking it in place, perhaps even gluing it or taping it with masking tape. You don't have to have the whole hull shaped at once; you can lay and resin parts of the section at a time, butting edges and leaving a strip unresined at the butt to pay into the new work.

Both Clark Craft and Glen-L offer all mentioned materials and free catalogues listing them. Specify fiberglass materials when writing. Complete building instructions are listed in *C-Flex*, Seemann Plastics, Inc., P.O. Box 13704, New Orleans, LA 70185, $7. PVC foam construction is described in *Foam Sandwich Boatbuilding*, Peter Wynn, $9 from International Marine Publishing Co., Camden, ME 04843.

Coast Guard Regulations

If you build a boat yourself, either one of your own design or from a kit, you are considered a manufacturer. As such, you must furnish a capacity plate that will state the maximum safe load, maximum safe horsepower, and proper amount of flotation. If the boat is under 20 feet, it must be capable of floating in an upright position with the maximum load on board. The U.S. Coast Guard issues a free publication (CGO-466 — *Safety Standards for Backyard Boat Builders*) that explains the measurements and provides all the formulas you need. Write to the Department of Transportation, U.S. Coast Guard, Washington, D.C., 20590.

8
Hunting Boats in General

All my life I've had a runaway love affair with hunting boats. Sneakboxes and sneakboats. Hunting garveys. Pushboats. All sizes, shapes, and descriptions. Hunting boats are better than other boats. They do double duty. A dinghy I had got painted white in spring to ferry me out to a bugeye I owned at the time. In the fall, a coat of duckboat brown went on the outside and I and another gunner went on the inside. Another sneakbox served as a small sailboat in hot weather and a duck machine in cold weather. My partner and I sat on either side of the centerboard. I wander from my subject, but I must tell you that one of the grandest sights I ever witnessed happened aboard this vessel when a flock of perhaps 300 broadbills swerved over the boat and decoys. My partner and I were spellbound by the awesome numbers. I can still hear the roar of their wings. At the finish, four birds trailed behind the huge flock. In formation they split, two down my partner's side of the boat, two down my side. It was as if we had directed their flight to create a dramatic climax to the unbelievable event.

Back to the subject, I was up to my old tricks knocking around the back alleys of shooting-fishing spots when I came upon a builder showing off a nifty little plywood hunting boat. "Is there a name for that kind of boat?" I asked him. "Ayup," said he in the thick accent of down-bay. "That there be a *ponebox*." It took me a week to figure out that what he had said was "pondbox." That is, a light, small boat capable of being dragged across the meadows and hidden at the edge of the small ponds black ducks love.

It was typical of what most hunting boats are and how they come to be. A hunting boat is shaped by dozens of simultaneous requirements: the size of the waters it is to be used on; whether it must carry the gunner to and from the shooting area or stays in one spot and serves as shelter and hide; maybe the boat must be grassed over; or perhaps the thick local cover affords ready concealment.

What kind of game is under attack is also involved in the design. Deer and moose get belted from boats in many places. A canoe may be perfect for the task. There are now, once again, tiny canoes weighing 20 to 30 pounds that can be carried in and out of rugged country. Rails and snipe in many places are attacked by special vessels called pushboats because the sternman must physically horse them through thick grasses by shoving on the bottom with a long pole. And even though standard-sized canoes are the world's tippiest boat, they too can be customized for handling railbird assignments.

The same canoe or johnboat that sports you after summer smallmouths may be a float boat for squirrel on fine fall mornings and hidden in a marsh bayou that afternoon. It's all a matter of knowing where and how to use them and customizing them to your needs.

Putting a boat into your hunting plans makes sense for a variety of reasons. The first is basic. Water and game have always tended to go together. Ducks and geese obviously require water for their existence. But all kinds of game tend to congregate around swamps, streams, rivers, and lakes. Vegetation is lusher, cover thicker, food more plentiful. Using some sort of craft to aid in hunting such places probably goes back to a caveman hanging on a log. As we'll see, a variety of ingenious boats have been developed to suit the differing requirements of water and hunting conditions.

Hunting from boats is a part of today's outdoor world and will be on the increase in tomorrow's. To understand why, some background information is needed. To begin with, most game populations are on the increase. This is spectacularly true of deer, Canada geese, and wild turkey. But everywhere modern management techniques are paying off. And they have to. More people are hunting than ever before. And they are tending to take less time to do it. The long leisurely hunts of yesterday are disappearing. Today's hunt is a quick trip in, a fast hunt, and out.

Here I am bundled up against the cold. The Zackbox is aluminum and many times has been used as an icebreaker for other boats.

There is a safety device on the bow of my Zackbox. I went swimming one icy night when another boat went adrift. After that the anchor was always on deck secured by a piece of shock cord. Whenever I went ashore the anchor did too.

And people are tending to expand their outdoor horizons. The camper buys a boat that he uses for fishing, which gets him interested in skin diving, etc. Those who like the outdoors are tending to stay in it all year round in one way or another. They've got a little time...most of the time.

Hunting is frequently a cold-weather sport, and there are some special considerations to using a boat in freezing temperatures. Motors today pose no problems. It's sheer wonder the way a properly tuned outboard starts even with temperatures in the cellar. In this kind of freezing weather, never tip your outboard up. Leave the lower unit straight up and down in the water. Tipping can leave water in the powerhead. In the up-and-down position all the water drains. Inboard or inboard/outboards must be drained or treated with antifreeze to avoid freezing problems. If you're doing a lot of winter work it's no trick to rig extension nipples on the drains so they are more easily accessible. Always check to see that they aren't clogged with sand or dirt.

Another concession you'll have to make to cold-weather hunting regards ice — the possibility of having to drive the boat through ice on the surface and the possibility that standing water will freeze in the boat if you leave it in the water. Water freezing in a round-bottomed boat probably won't harm it since the ice will push up the sides. A square-sided boat is okay, too, as long as the ice does not get a good purchase on both sides. Two inches of water or more above the chine line is the danger zone. It may spring the side planks. Temperatures have to go down and stay down to do this, but it has happened. The solution is to keep your boat covered. If this isn't possible, a pound or two of rock salt in the bottom will sap the ice of its strength.

Running through ice also holds some hazards. Curiously, skim ice is far more likely to damage a wood boat than thick ice. Broken ice from ½ inch to several inches thick will just be pushed aside as you run the boat through it. (Naturally, you don't run fast under these conditions.) You can even blaze a trail through unbroken ice a couple of inches thick without damaging your boat. The trick is to keep the bow running on top of the ice. The weight of the boat amidships crushes and separates the ice.

Skim ice has a cutting edge. Running through it can saw through the leading water-line sections of wood planking. If your boat is fiberglass, fiberglass over wood, or aluminum, there's no danger. Ice won't harm any of these. If your boat is wood, sheathe waterline surfaces with wood pieces you can replace when chewed up or with thin sheets of aluminum or galvanized steel tacked over the planks.

And don't worry inordinately. Despite the horrible tales you may hear, you've got to plow up a considerable amount of icewater before any serious damage results. Look over the commercial boats in your area. If they aren't protected, forget it.

But while we are in the general area, a word about safety. It's important, always, of course. It is even more so in cold-weather, cold-water boating. See that your fire extinguishers work. Under no circumstances forget matches, and a lighter with lighter fluid and flints is better. Gasoline will start the wettest wood. Wear wool clothes or new foam-insulation garments; they stay warm when wet. And don't get wet! Wear wet-weather gear and stay in the boat.

While the backyard-variety outboard is a fine boat to provide access to hunting areas, it's high time we started talking about more specific hunting designs. Let's take them one by one.

Canoes

This small ship is unquestionably one of the finest hunting boats ever created, as its reputation would tend to attest. There is no need to dwell here on its rich history nor the arduous journeys that stand everlastingly to the credit of its sturdy design. The canoe's safe, easily powered hull shape can be seen in the dugouts of native craft around the world. Formerly sailed and/or paddled only, even in remote regions, its stern has been bobbed to take a small outboard motor. Although not fast, the outboard canoe has a multiplicity of virtues. It is strong but light, a necessity where portages over land are involved. It can carry heavy loads without sacrifice of sea ability. Even when loaded it still moves through the water easily, resulting in economy of operation—important in areas where gasoline is expensive and fueling docks few and far between.

With several important exceptions, it is almost always used as an access boat. Hunters get "back in" by canoe. But in the north where the aquatic-loving moose is king, hunters often ghost along the shoreline in a canoe, the guide silently paddling, the hunter ready in the bow.

Another important exception makes the canoe a prime hunting boat for anyone. It is unbeatable for the float hunt. This kind of hunt is exactly what the name implies. Hunters float silently down a stream shooting at game flushed by the presence of the boat. The quarry is most often ducks. But squirrels, crows, or woodchucks might be in the sights. Even deer at morning or evening when they may be using the stream to water are within reach of floating hunters if local laws allow.

Under certain conditions floating becomes the very best way of all to hunt ducks. That's when it has been cold enough to freeze lakes and ponds but the moving water of streams and rivers remains open. The birds are forced out of the thousand little potholes they hide in and must take to open water.

On deepwater streams where launching areas are strategically located, there is no reason why you couldn't float-hunt from your outboard. Unfortunately, these conditions seldom appear. Usually some lifting over shoals or in and out is required — and here the canoe comes into its own. Outboard-equipped, you can run quickly through unproductive areas, then take up the silent paddle to stalk the thickly brushed spots where game hides.

Deck adds to rough-water ability in this small canoe.

This Ozark johnboat is in action on the Current River. A somewhat crudely built local vessel.

Modified Johnboats

Another float boat developed primarily for fishing the broad shallow streams of the southwest is the johnboat. In its traditional design, it is a flat-bottomed craft, with a square sea-sled bow and stern. The best qualities of its design have been adapted by several manufacturers, who have shortened the length and conserved weight by aluminum construction. While it is not as easily paddled as a canoe, its broad bottom provides a more stable shooting platform and it can be powered with a much larger outboard for faster speeds. Although not as easy to carry as the canoe, two men can handle one with ease. Other conventional aluminum boats in 12- to 14-foot size are also fine float-hunt craft because of their light weight.

There aren't many ways to customize a boat for float hunts. You might rig a notch to hold your gun in bumpy stretches. An old float trick is to tie a line to the paddle so you can drop it to shoot and not have to place it inside the boat. A trick I use on summer floats is to tie things in a plastic bag — a canoe bag is better, but I don't have one — and lash the bag to the crossbrace. I always keep my tackle box closed so it will float free in a capsize. I think I'd rig a lashing system for my shotgun as well so when I was the offman, it would stick with the boat in a capsize.

Who shoots, incidentally, in a float depends on how safe you are. Certainly the stern must turn down many shots. If you and your partner are cool hands, birds flaring sideways or up might allow both shooters to take a crack at them. Some floaters downright forbid the sternman to lay a hand on his gun and the two shift off positions.

Duckboats

Duckboats gawdalmighty. Just the thought of them sets me shaking. Happens every fall. I get duckboat seizures. If I'm affluent, I buy one. If I'm broke, I build one. In between I bring the season in by fussing over the fleet. At one point I had five duckboats in the backyard—two coffinboxes, a pondbox, a sneakbox, and the Zackbox. Others had astonishing things to say about the clutter of battered mud-colored veterans. Only to a duck hunter are they beautiful.

Duckboats. Okay. Let's start off on the wrong foot. It's hard to find a good duckboat. Although the hunters who want them want them badly, they aren't bought in sufficient quantity for the large manufacturers to keep them in production. For example, both Lund and Aluma-Craft used to make nifty little duckboats out of aluminum. They were expensive (around $375), but thousands were bought. Both, alas, are now discontinued. All of which is why I guess you see so many different kinds of boats pressed into duckboat service. Canoes. Rubber rafts. Cement-mixing boxes. All faithfully camouflaged. Some work okay. Others swamp or sink or flip and kill somebody.

The result is that duckboats with few exceptions are built by small, regional builders. A guy gets an idea for a boat that he wants for himself. He builds it. Others see him coming home with an inordinate amount of game and clamor to have a boat for themselves. Since the original guy has a yen for boatbuilding anyway, he complies. The first thing you know he's in the boat biz. However, *staying* a boatbuilder—i.e., making any money—is an extremely tough thing to do, and so builders come and go. What adds more difficulty and price is that while Aluma-Craft, say, could throw a ducker on a truckload shipment and keep costs reasonable, if you want a boat from this regional guy you either drive to get the boat yourself or pay an enormous freight bill to have it crated and shipped to you.

Access Boats

First off, when you talk about hunting boats you must divide them into three categories. Access boats take you to hunting areas. Then there are boats you actually hunt out of. Finally, there are vessels that accomplish both purposes. Let's take the first kind.

Plenty of hunters use their regular runabouts in summertime colors to get them beyond the crowds. Down my way, Chesapeake Bay is cluttered with islands and hard-to-get-to peninsulas. A boat gives easy access to all. You'll find deer hunters in the west and midwest running down lakes and rivers to get to prime deer or squirrel covers that may be almost impossible to reach any other way. A few hunters in the south use houseboats as access vessels and actually camp out on them during duck or deer season.

Aluminum Cartoppers

Both johnboats and sharp-bowed runabouts make fine hunting boats. I see guys all the time camouflaging them with nets for duck hunting. They can be very fast. And they are so light you can drag one across a marsh or up a bank with ease and conceal it with natural cover.

Lots of different companies build these boats. You don't want one too big — 12 or 14 feet. Grumman has recently brought out a nice level-flotation aluminum in a 12-foot version at around $950 and in a 14½-foot version at $1,400. Sears' old Gamefisher was a great duckboat, and their new tri-hull is even better — a 12-foot version for $700 and a 14-foot version for $950. On the smaller side, it's somewhat hard to find johnboats in the 10-foot range. At this writing, Smoker-Craft, New Paris, IN 46553, has an 8-footer at 52 pounds and 41-inch beam. This should fit in the back of standard-size station wagons.

Duckboats in General

There are all the reasons in the world why you should rig a boat especially for duck hunting. As mentioned, it puts you beyond the crowd, gives you an edge. Second, it is

A light aluminum in action.

Obviously a sneakbox was the original inspiration for this ducker. Hinged lids close the cockpit.

a safe and versatile way to hunt. With your boat stowed on a trailer, you can hunt one place one day, another the next. You can follow the birds. Your rig comes home every night and sits safe in your yard. You aren't surprised by the theft of a decoy spread or outboard in midseason.

Another reason for boat hunting is the increasingly stringent land restrictions. With a boat you are seldom in any one place long enough to arouse any landowner's ire, as might be the case if he found you'd built a blind on his property without permission. Even if land is posted, there may well be grassy areas out from shore that could hide your boat. With no contact with shore, you have every right to set up where you please. (I might caution that riparian-rights laws. trespass laws, and even laws governing blinds are different everywhere. Better check carefully if you want to put this to a test.)

Public hunting areas are on the increase everywhere. Here again, you'd hesitate to build a permanent blind because even if it escaped being vandalized in your absence, you could often expect to find it occupied by other hunters. What happens in this confrontation depends on those concerned, but it would seem likely no good could arise from the situation. A boat does away with the problem.

I hunted last season in Virginia, where all the marshland in the state belongs to the state; thus, it's okay for anyone to build a blind where he pleases. Okay so far. My host gunned from an elaborate stake blind. He'd sunk pilings and built a houselike box on them, which he grassed over with fresh-cut cedar trees. To duplicate it would prob-

I've started several boats like this. Cut down the sides of any rowboat, then deck it. Burlap covering makes good concealment and, unlike most grassing jobs, the boat can still be trailed at high speed.

ably cost $200 minimum, using scrap materials, and take several days' labor by at least two people. While we hunted, an oyster tonger came in and began working right off the decoys—scaring away any ducks, of course. Did my host say anything? No sir. If he had, he could have expected to come out next time and find his blind burned down. It has happened to his buddy the week before. More reason to boat-hunt.

AlumaCraft made this neat little "ducker." Great little hide boat or a boat to slide into a pond. You find them sometimes on the used market. (Courtesy Aluma Craft Boat Assoc., Alpex Corp., Minneapolis, Minn.)

For all of it, I think the versatility of a hunting boat is its greatest attribute. The very nature of waterfowling is changing as modern game biology becomes more and more sophisticated. Special seasons, bag limits restricted or relaxed, areas opened or closed suddenly without warning—these practices are increasing. The one-place, one-species concept will penalize any waterfowler more and more. For example, every modern waterfowler should be turning himself into the Ph.D. of waterfowlers—a goose hunter. Everywhere in the nation, Canada geese are increasing at a staggering rate. (I wish I could say they were getting dumber!) Blues and snow geese are also holding up well; snows are legal to hunt on the Atlantic flyway again after seasons were shut down in 1931! With a boat you can get after them one day, ducks the next. If mallards are restricted one year, take the mallard decoys out of the boat and stock for teal. Or geese. Or coots. Or broadbills.

Legal and Illegal

The first consideration in boat hunting is legality. One kind of boat hunting that is illegal by federal standards is the sinkbox or battery. Nowadays it is almost impossible to find an old battery, and even the cast-iron decoys are collector's items. However, a buddy of mine once considered making a boat blind that would in effect be an artificial point and look like a piece of marsh. He planned to build big wing tanks into which he would pump water to sink the whole rig deeper. It would probably have been considered illegal as a form of sinkbox.

By now you are probably thinking about getting way out in the water with boat or boatblind. While it is no longer a federal law that you must anchor your boat within 100 feet from shore, most states still retain this law. Check the laws of the state where you plan to hunt.

Widely misunderstood (because they are relatively new) are laws relating to outboards on boats. You no longer have to remove your motor when shooting; the law says only that your boat must be immobile. You *can* use the outboard (or sail) to retrieve cripples; you can also shoot cripples from the power-operated boat if the motor is shut off. This is a good ruling since everybody did it anyway except no one shut off the engine. You can row, scull, or paddle a boat after waterfowl. Again, state laws may differ.

Open-Water Boats

After we divide the boats that are outlawed from legal hunting boats, it is necessary to make another distinction. Boats used for diving ducks (canvasback and redheads, where legal, greater and lesser scaup) must be anchored in open water where these species generally feed. Since the ducks dive for food, the depth of water can be from a few feet up to as much as 20 feet. And not only are these ducks less wary as species than the most popular puddle ducks, blacks and mallards, but the fact that they are away from shore also decreases their natural wariness. What this means to you is that you need a larger boat, although much less, even crude, concealment can be employed. My

The Zackbox inspired this vessel. Here she is framed up according to the plans. Dimensions were altered slightly because the Zackbox as drawn on plans wouldn't come up the builder's cellarway.

Boat is planked out. Decoy hatch shows clearly here.

This is a conversion of a Starcraft aluminum 16-foot fishing boat into a duckboat. First, a forward casting platform that was on the floor was torn out.

Second, the decks were widened. Strips were tied into bow deck with bolts and covered with plywood.

A watertight bulkhead was installed forward of the laydown portion of the cockpit. A hatch cover keeps decoys lockable.

The boat was camouflaged; the open cockpit shows the boat's roominess. Speed is great with a large outboard. Conversion was done by members of the Old Duck Hunters of Connecticut.

experience, especially with broadbills (scaup), is that in a rainstorm or snowstorm you could shoot them from any boat with no concealment. In fact I've heard of a fellow on Long Island Sound who drapes burlap bags over his boat and shoots the ducks from the stern cockpit. His boat is a 25-foot twin-engined Bertram. I shoot scoters and old-squaws from my 20-foot Wellcraft without camouflage of any kind.

Almost any boat can qualify for this duty, and the deciding factor is probably the suitability of the boat for the waters. If you are in big water you need something substantial, a husky rowboat with a 20-hp motor. The flatties get used a lot because their great stability makes a good shooting platform and their freeboard and silhouette are low. Don't forget, you will want to be hunting in the worst weather, in storm and wind, so gauge your boat accordingly.

Your cover for your boat is limited only by your ingenuity. A burlap bag over the motor is universal. Grass, small cedars, rushes, and branches on a small frame that attaches at the sides are best. But you can use burlap or camouflage net too. What you want is to merely conceal the human figures inside.

Floating blinds are used in some places. The disadvantage of them — beyond cost — is that if you moor them permanently they are subject to damage in the ice, floods, and storms that can be expected everywhere in fall and winter. They either sink, break loose, or are torn up. And they too get burned up some places. If you can overcome all these obstacles, they can be made roomy and comfortable.

Hide Boats for Puddle Ducks

Following an intensive survey, I have found that every possible kind of boat that could conceivably be used to shoot puddle ducks from has been used not once but many times. This includes prams, canoes, cartoppers, airboats, johnboats, fiberglass utilities, and inflatables. You name it; somebody is using it. In fact about the only waterborne vehicle I haven't seen being used as a duckboat is a surfboard, and I'm almost afraid to mention it for fear that may be next. However, none of the above really fills the bill the way it should. A real duckboat has a variety of requirements. Let's look at them in detail.

HULL DESIGN. This isn't as important as some of the other requirements, and all kinds of johnboats and sharp-ended rowboat-like hulls are in use. You want flat bottom and beam so the boat can handle shallow water. Lightness is important, because you'll be dragging it up and down banks, and lack of weight, coupled with the flat after sections, will make the boat plane easily with the 6-hp and maybe with the little 4-hp. (She'll fly with the 9½-hp.) Under 9 feet gets too small to lay out in properly, and larger than 13 feet gets into the two-man size. The very best hull design is a gently curved bottom because it sits you down deepest in the boat and sits the boat deeper in the water, even more lowering the silhouette.

FULL-DECKED HULL. It is essential to have the boat fully decked for various reasons. If the going gets rough, she'll stick her nose into big seas. The deck will throw the water off. Warmth is important to the waterfowler. In bitter cold and wind, a full deck keeps you warm. Old-timers put a kerosene lantern at either end to add some fire. One of the small catalytic heaters would be even better.

Another reason for the deck, coupled with the hatch, is that you can close up the boat to rain, sleet, hail, and snakes in the south and leave her parked somewhere without having to worry about a storm filling it. And with the hasp, you can lock decoys and gear inside. Of course, villains could chop a hole in the cover, but you seldom find thieves going that far.

You can build your deck flat. It builds easier that way, but it makes the boat higher and bulkier. Also a curve throws the ends of the grass down over the sides, and this helps hide the boat.

DECOY RACKS. At turnpike trailer speeds, you should stow your decoys inside when running to and from the marsh because they may bounce or blow off. But when picking up or putting the blocks out, it saves time and trouble to stow them on the afterdeck first.

OARS. You need them for maneuvering around the decoys, and as a safety factor. They may bring you home late, but that is preferable to spending the night in the marsh.

INTERIOR SHELVES. Two small shelves that are easy to reach put your gear in the proper place. Make deep rails on the edges of the shelves so the gear will stay put when traveling on bumpy roads. Don't leave your gun in the boat when you trailer, incidentally. The vibration can quickly rub the bluing off even if the weapon is in a case.

The Zackbox in use as a hide boat. There was deep enough water in this little gut to float her, and high banks on either side kept the 15-foot hull hidden.

COCKPIT AND DECK SIZES. There will be times when cripples are down or when you're out of the boat and hear *honk, honk, honk* and you want to get in FAST. In those situations, you need at least a 30-inch cockpit and a space between deck and bottom of 16 inches. Remember you'll be bundled up and booted when this vessel leaves port.

GRASS. I see boats being used that are just painted (with flat no-gloss brown paint only, of course), but I've always felt more comfortable with some grass on the boat.

The Boat in Use

If you've got a good boat it can be used for both access and concealment. It can take you from the launch area to your hunting grounds safely in all kinds of weather. (The more sheltered a route, the better off you are. Don't forget, when wind and storm are howling is when you'll want to be gunning. Often by utilizing shelters and lees, you can reach exposed points.) After you get your decoys out, hide the boat, using whatever natural cover is available. It becomes your blind or hide. If the shore is rocky, pile some rocks around the boat. If it is sandy, maybe you can dig a little hole for it. You'd be surprised at how digging a grassed-up boat into the sand as little as six inches makes it disappear. Walk 30 feet from it and you can barely see it. If you are hunting a marsh, the little drains or ditches carved out by the tide make fine hides during all but the last couple hours of high tide. If there is natural high grass, slide the boat into the grass. Some river bars or banks or exposed shores collect lots of flotsam and jetsam. Slide the boat up the shore and throw whatever is there around and on the boat, even if it's old logs, planks, brush. The important thing is to make the boat blend in with the surroundings.

High storm tides are the boat hunter's bugaboo. If the whole marsh is flooded, it may well be that you can't gun your regular spots because the water is so high the boat can't be hidden in any natural grass. In that case, abandon your regular spots and seek new ones. Although some areas would not normally be watercovered, the high tide turns them into new ducking spots. Bushes and trees that are normally too high can now be used as cover because of the high water. Draw the boat into them. With some ingenuity and effort, you can usually find some cover somewhere. What you've got going for you is that the unusual high water will also put the ducks on the prowl. They won't like it either; the strangeness and novelty will frighten them. As in high winds they will trade more and seek the security of their own kind more. Both factors will tend to make them decoy to spreads in odd places. What every puddle duck longs for is a nice balmy day with the temperature in the low 40s, a modest wind, and a place where he can feed or rest in near or total concealment. Those are the days *not* to gun.

9
Specific Hunting Designs

The Barnegat sneakbox and its first cousin, the Long Island scooter, are among the all-time great duck-hunting boats. Both are hunting machines unparalleled for crossing choppy open water and then, as the name implies, sneaking into a hiding spot on a marshy point or pond. Both sneakbox and scooter are round-bottomed craft, stub-nosed with a broad stern and rounded deck. A small cockpit holds one hunter (a few two-man boats were built). Other unique features are removable racks on the stern to hold decoys and a long dagger centerboard that can be thrust into the soft bay bottom to hold the boat in position when decoys are set or retrieved.

Like the canoe, these boats have a hull form that permits them to be rowed long distances without tiring the oarsman. Originally designed for sail, most traditional "boxes" are now equipped with outboard brackets. They can utilize the power of only the smallest motors, however, and top speeds are low. When long distances are involved, the boats are usually towed by a larger boat. Other disadvantages are heavy weight for their size and a complicated design that makes them relatively expensive to build. However, they last a long time. Many a fifty-year-old veteran still sees service on the marshes.

The Zackbox

The Barnegat sneakbox was the grandest duck-killing machine ever made right up to the time they made high-horsepower outboards cheap, light, and utterly dependable. I'll admit it is downright uppity even for a know-it-all like me to knock a boat that did its job so perfectly for 132 years. But the truth is, it's obsolete.

You see, the sneakbox was designed to be rowed or sailed. Its rounded curves won't take outboard motors bigger than about 5 hp, and with one of them you won't get from one point to another much faster than your grandpappy. That was okay for him. There were a lot more ducks, far fewer hunters, and lots of places to gun near cities

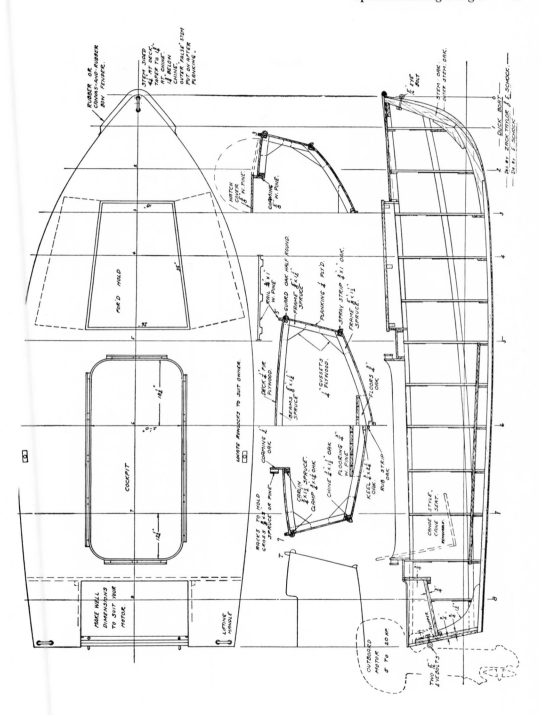

THE ZACKBOX

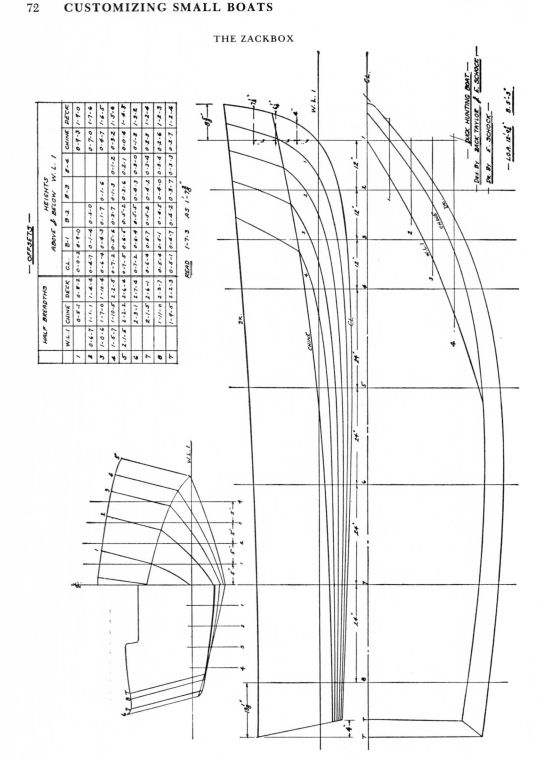

and towns. Today the ducks are usually a far piece away, and the nearby hot spots fill up fast. To get there first you need performance. You need a boat that can rival a broadbill with the wind on its tail and still be safe, seaworthy, and dry. It's no trick to achieve this today if you talk in terms of motors from 10 to 35 hp (still light enough for one-man portability). Any cartopper with a 10-hp will do it. What is sorely wanting is a blend of the old and new. Today's duck hunter needs the planing hull of the runabout. And he is cheerfully willing to sacrifice the sneakbox's sailing and rowing ability to get it. Yet who wants to sacrifice the unique and wholly magnificent features that made sneakboxes the finest duckboats ever? To see what those features were and how they operated, let's take an excursion into history and see how grandpappy used his boat to kill ducks.

In the first place, he didn't baby it. The boat could take care of itself. It lived outdoors. A deck and watertight hatch kept it dry through the severest storms. When decoys were picked up, they were stored breast down on the afterdeck and they stayed there until they went overboard again. Grandpa didn't even wrap the lines — just let 'em string out.

He watched where the birds were working. Then he would slip out there, rowing if it was a short ways (that is, a couple miles), sailing if more and if the wind was fair. (The sail and mast were short enough to stow in the boat.) He'd find a pond, sheltered guzzle, or good point and toss out decoys. Then his practiced eye would seek a hide. It might be a mosquito ditch, a clump of grass, or even a rough background. The old boy would pull his boat in there, taking care to cover the decks with grass from the immediate area (the real secret). Then he'd slip down out of sight, hat over the eyes, his head against a padded board, and wait for the fun to begin.

The Zackbox is a sneakbox for modern gunning. Essentially it can do everything the boats of old could do, and it adds a wrinkle or two of its own. Let's look at what makes this a duck killer of such awesome proportions. Since nobody is offering this boat commercially, you may have to build one up for yourself or modify an existing vessel. These are the features you need.

HULL. Any high-speed hull will do. The beamier the better since it will be more stable and draw less water. No deep V; too much draft. It should be as light and strong as possible. For a one-man boat, 12 feet is perfect. The present boat is two-man at 14 feet. Hull material should be aluminum, fiberglass, or glass over wood for protection from the ice.

MOTOR. The minimum is 10 hp. This will give you 20 mph in a 12-footer. A 20-hp will push a 14-footer over 20 mph. If the hull will take it, a 35-hp can be used, but its weight of 135 pounds or so is the outside limit. Heavier than this and the boat simply gets too heavy to drag into a hide. In action, the motor is tipped up and a burlap sack is thrown over it. The motor should sit in a self-bailing well cut into the afterdeck. You'll want to equip your boat with oarlocks and oars because it is often easier to row to pick up the decoys. The oars also serve as emergency power, but any planing boat is cranky and tiresome to row very far.

DECK. A full deck is needed for a variety of reasons. In my opinion any boat without one *can't* be a real duck machine. The deck makes the boat warm and dry in all weather. (You should be able to get right inside the boat and sleep in it if necessary.) Also of great importance is the fact that the deck holds the concealing grass and hides the man. Last but not least, it makes the boat and its contents completely invisible, watertight, and lockable. On my Zackbox the deck is flat, which is preferable to no deck at all and easier to build than a rounded deck. However, it is better to have a rounded deck with about a 4-inch crown. This lowers the profile, and, more important, it throws the ends of the concealing grass downward, helping to cover the sides.

HATCH. The hatch should be at least 2 feet forward of the transom so your weight never leaves the center of the boat. You may gun out of the boat while it is floating, and you don't want one end sticking up. Don't make the hatch opening too big — 2 by 3 feet is okay for one man, 2 by 4 feet for two men. The hatch should have a cover. You can toss this aside when you gun. In bad weather, draw it up to your chin and it will help keep you warm. I hinged the 4-foot hatch of my box in the middle so it folds flat and it made it much less clumsy.

LOW SILHOUETTE. The old duck principle of nothing sticking up is good and less than that is even better because it keeps the boat's freeboard at a minimum. (You don't worry about an errant wave coming aboard since the deck and outboard will throw it off.) Actually the length of your booted foot decides the height of the deck. Your foot must be able to rest upright. Lying splayfooted is uncomfortable. Add a couple of inches so you can slide in and out relatively easily and you have your height. My insulated, big-booted foot measures 15 inches, so my boat's freeboard is about 17 inches. If I had a round deck, the sides could be lowered 4 inches.

LOCKABILITY. You want water and people locked out of your boat. Even if you don't store it in the marsh this is important. You can trailer in storms and know no water is going in the boat. Mine sits outside all season long and thrives on it. The motor can be locked with a bicycle lock through the clamp handles, but it is even better to stow the motor out of sight inside. The gas tank stays inside under the afterdeck. Its line leads to the motor through a small hole in the well. A strong brass hook at one end of the cover and a hasp at the other make an effective locking arrangement.

DECOY STORAGE. If you don't trailer the boat, you can store decoys on the deck in the old tradition. If so, simply make removable boards about 6 inches high around the afterdeck. If you trailer, there is too much jumping around for this. My decoys are stored out of sight in a special compartment under the forward deck. You can stow gear here by reaching in from the cockpit, but a hinged door in the deck is convenient because you can then pick up the decoys from the water and position them in place without having to climb aboard. Using every available inch, my boat now holds exactly fifty oversize Canada goose decoys.

COMFORT AND SAFETY. Flotation is called for even with fiberglass-covered plywood construction. Position sheets in the bilge and cover with a plywood panel that is flat and at least 6 feet long. Tuck this floor into the corners carefully so you don't lose small stuff, and carry it to the transom under the afterdeck for the same reason. You can sit/lie on a preserver cushion, but usually you are so heavily clothed it isn't necessary. I rig lines that hold the oars up out of the way against the deck. Shells, lunch, supply bag, flashlight, and sundry gear stay on the side out of the way. (And really stay there. Only my gun and lunch thermos leave the boat at night.)

TRAILERABILITY. You'll need a bow that slopes enough to climb a trailer easily and a low bow eye.

Here's another trick you should use on all small boats. For launching or tying the boat up you need a painter. Measure it off from the bow eye or cleat to exactly 6 inches too short to foul the propeller if it goes overboard, which it will do often enough. Actually I run the Zackbox a good deal while standing and hold onto this painter to help from getting tossed overboard accidentally. So far it has worked.

Since by now you should be convinced that every redblooded American boy should have a Zackbox he can call his own, the question arises as to how to go about getting it. You can build one from the plans shown here or have a builder do it. You can take an existing hull and fit it out yourself, which is a neat way to do it. Or you can hope that some manufacturer will think he can sell enough of them to build one like it. I hope not. Too many duck killers like it around and they'll have to cut down bag limits again.

Plywood Sneakbox

The Wigeon is not a true sneakbox, for old baymen will tell you that these boats should have "clean-swept chines," meaning that the bottom and crowned deck timbers as well as the curve of the chine are all arcs of circles. Our boat is a modified

Decoy racks and a spray shield give this little Widgeon a salty look.

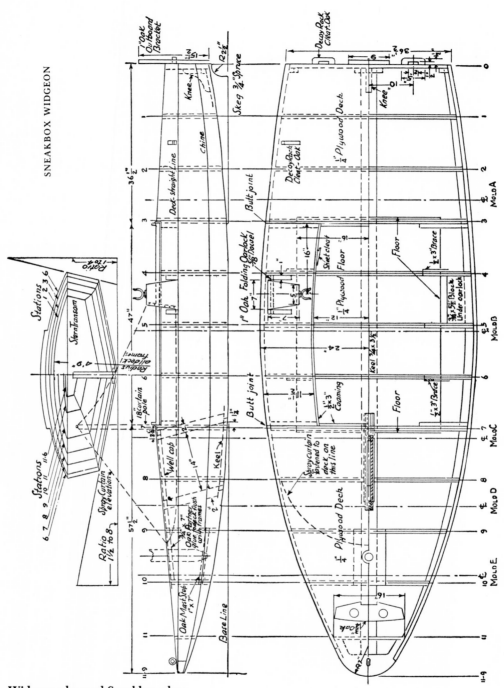

Widgeon plywood Sneakbox plans.

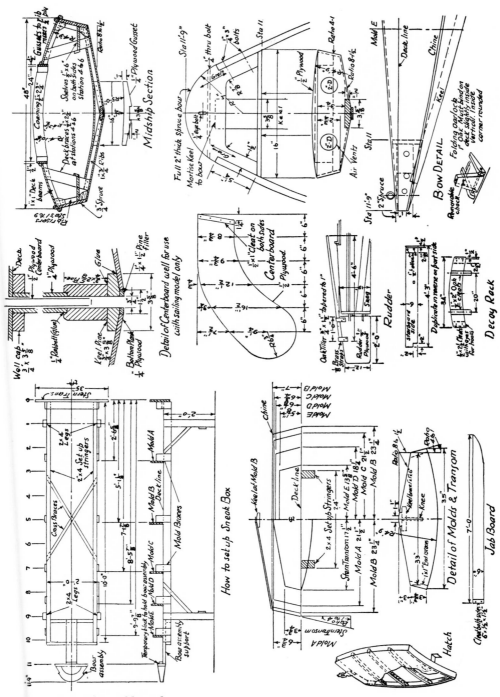

Widgeon plywood Sneakbox plans.

sneakbox with dead-rise sides and a V bottom. It is designed for simplicity of construction with plywood, which cannot be bent into the compound curves of a true sneakbox.

Because it is made out of plywood, which requires careful alignment, the plan calls for "setting up" substantial 2-by-4 stringers on which molds are located. The boat is built bottom up and then turned over to construct the deck.

The setup plan has legs at a convenient height from the floor, but if you have a substantial pair of horses, the legs may be dispensed with. By all means, build the setup form accurately and make sure that it is square at the four corners before nailing the diagonal crossbraces. Note that the stern transom and the bow assembly are the only pieces in the setup that remain in the finished boat. Lay off the indicated distances for each mold and nail the mold braces in place to receive them. The molds are cut from second 1-inch planks such as 7-inch-wide shelving. Be sure, however, that the lumber selected for both molds and setup stringers is not warped because your success depends on these forms being accurately sized, aligned, and placed. Fasten molds to the mold braces with screws so that they may be easily removed at the proper time.

Note on the plans that the line where the side planks and deck meet (the deckline) is a straight line running fore and aft. Always keep this in mind because it is an essential reference line. At the deckline, cut notches in each mold that will take $7/8 \times 1$-inch strips extending from bow to stern on both sides. These must form a straight line, and if they do not, molds must be corrected. When the side planks are in position, these strips are used to scribe the deckline on the planks.

Note that the angle the sides make with the vertical is the same for all the molds and for the stern transom as well. It is a diagonal in the ratio 1:4. I suggest that you make a very accurate pattern cut at this angle to be used in making all molds. For convenience in attaching clamps to hold side planks, nail a 1-inch-square batten to the end of each mold.

A stern transom is formed from $7/8$-inch spruce or pine. At the deck, its curvature is the arc of a circle whose diameter is 57 inches. To draw this and other curves, make your own beam compass from a $1 \times 1/2$-inch batten, 5 feet long, with a pencil stub set in one end and a brad driven in as a pivot at the proper radial distance.

Having laid this arc off and drawn the chord, which is 35 inches, draw the side angles with your 1:4 pattern. The angle of the V bottom is $1 1/2 : 8$, and this should be laid off directly on the transom, as indicated on the detail plan. After the transom has been shaped, glue and screw pieces of 1×1-inch oak flush along the ends and also the $1 \times 1 \times 6$-inch oak strip to which the keel is fastened so that the keel will be flush with the transom. Like the molds, the transom is set at a right angle to the setup stringers and is temporarily fastened to the braces with screws.

Bow assembly is shown in precise detail on the plan. Rough out the nosepieces, but leave out final shape-up until ribs and deck frames are in place, after which you can determine with a straightedge just how much trimming is needed. Temporarily screw bow assembly to the setup form, making sure that it is properly aligned. Now you are ready to start actual construction. You will need two $3/4$-inch side planks, 8 inches wide and 12 feet long. My preference would be white cedar boat boards, but clear spruce or pine is good. Start by clamping the planks at the stern by applying pressure at the opposite end with a rope tourniquet. Proceeding from the stern, clamp both planks to opposite sides of each mold. As you go toward the bow, spring the boards gradually with the tourniquet until they are flush with the bow assembly. In this way you will avoid unequal pressure that might pull your molds slightly out of line. Now clamp $1 \times \frac{1}{2}$-inch battens, 12 feet long, along the molds at the chine lines and draw these lines on the side planks. Scribe the decklines as indicated above. Saw the planks to shape, allowing at least ⅛ inch top and bottom to be planed down. The planks should be identical. Now clamp them together and plane down to exact size. Reclamp them to the molds, using the same procedure outlined above. At the stern the planks are permanently glued and screwed to the transom, and at the bow, glued and bolted to the assembly. The bottom frames or ribs are 1-inch deep by ¾-inch wide cedar or spruce and are joined at the center with ⅜-inch plywood gusset, which is dimensioned on the detail sketch of the midship section. These rib assemblies are identical as to angle ($1\frac{1}{2}$:8) and vary only in length. Using a sheet of plywood (the piece you will use for the floor is okay), lay off a baseline 4 feet long and bisect it at right angles with a centerline. At the ends of the baseline, draw 4½-inch perpendiculars. From the centerline draw the two lines that subtend the right angles whose sides are 24 inches and 4½ inches (ratio 8:1½). On these lines, which form an obtuse angle, nail ¾ × 1½-inch battens. At their junction, with its ends touching the battens, center and nail a 3⅝ × ½-inch block that is 1¼ inches thick.

If you examine the detailed midship section, the above will be quite clear. This arrangement will provide you with a jig upon which to construct all the ribs. The ribs are mortised so that when laid along the battens they fit the keel block on the jig. Nail them temporarily in place and lay a gusset on them. Drill three screwholes on each side of the keel block, glue the gusset to the ribs, and screw it in place with ¾-inch No. 6 screws. Put gussets on both sides of the ribs. Make ten ribs to be installed at stations 1 to 10 inclusive. Make each one long enough to span the boat at its particular station. Ribs and deck frames are connected at stations 1 to 10 with ¾-inch to 1-inch rib risers (see midship section) and joined by small ¼-inch plywood gussets glued and screwed (only one gusset to each joint). Each rib riser is attached to the side planks with glue and two 1½-inch No. 7 screws.

Set one rib at station 6 and brace it firmly from the setup stringers in a vertical position, making sure that it is absolutely square across the boat with the keel notch exactly at the center. Prepare the keel, which is ¾ × 3⅝-inch pine or spruce, and bevel it as indicated. Fasten it permanently at the stern transom, bend it into the notch on the station 6 rib, and clamp it temporarily there and to the bow asembly. Working forward from the stern, set all ribs. They must go in place without forcing the keel out of line fore and aft. If additional arch in the keel is necessary, simply loosen clamps at station 6 and the bow. After securely fastening all ribs to the rib risers, glue the keel to the ribs. Next glue and screw to the center of the keel a ¼ × 1½-inch pine strip against which the bottom planks butt.

With ribs and keel in place, use a batten laid along the ribs as a guide in trimming the bottom of the bow assembly so that planking will fit snugly. Bevel the sides to conform to the rib angle. Temporarily attach a 2 × 1-foot sheet of ¼-inch marine plywood to the ribs. Lay the stern end of this sheet flush with the outside of the stern transom. The sheet is roughly marked along the keel and cut to shape and then carefully planed to fit along the keel exactly. With a few screws, temporarily fasten the sheet in place and scribe the line of the chine on it (where side plank meets the bottom sheet). Cut to this line, allowing at least ¼ inch to be planed down when the sheet is permanently installed. This sheet will serve as a pattern for the opposite side. Both are carefully fitted and glued to the planks, keel, and ribs. Space ¾-inch No. 6 screws 2 inches apart along side planks and keel and 4 inches apart on ribs. I recommend that you use a hard-setting resorcinol resin glue. If you plan to use an outboard with more than 3 hp, then use ⅜-inch plywood on the bottom. Then the thickness of the strip along the keel between the bottom planks must be increased to ⅜ inch. Fiberglass the bottom if desired.

The boat is now turned over to be decked, and the setup form is removed. All deck frames are sawed on a 57-inch outside radius, using the beam compass. Have the grain run tangent to the frame at the center. Frames are cut from a ¾-inch plank and are made 1¼ inches deep. They are set flush with the sides at stations 1 to 10 and rest on the rib risers, to which they are fastened with gussets as described above. Before you permanently fasten deck frames, set them temporarily and check for alignment. Lay a straightedge at the center of the frames from station 7 to the bow and one from station 3 to the stern transom. If your side planks have been properly shaped, each group of frames will be in perfect line. If not, you must correct the side planks to bring them into line. Bevel the side planks to conform to the curve of the frames. Also at this point trim any excess off the deck level of the bow assembly, so that the deck fits it. Note that at stations 3 and 7 the frames are double where the deck is butt-joined. If you plan a centerboard well, do not install frame 8 until the well cap is in place.

Although the finished boat will not have frames across the cockpit, install full frames from side to side at stations 4, 5, and 6. Leave them until you are ready to install the side decks from stations 3 to 7 and braces supporting the deck are in place. Temporarily nail a longitudinal strip to deck frames 3 to 7 close to those points where coaming will be installed. This will prevent lateral movement of the frames. Cut away frames 4, 5, and 6. On each side screw-fasten a ½ × 1½-inch strip extending from frames 3 to 7, its top flush with the deck frames. We will call these strips "cockpit liner." Glue the side decks and screw them to the side planks, cockpit liner, and frames with ¾-inch No. 6 screws. Save cutaway frames and use to construct a hatch.

Before going any further, let us consider several optional uses of the boat. If you plan to use her entirely with an outboard motor, you may dispense with the centerboard and well, mast hole and step, and rudder and sails. By all means retain the oarlocks and buy a stout pair of 7-foot ash oars, both for safety and for convenience. Should you decide to depend on your own brawn and the little winter sail for reaching when the wind blows fair, the centerboard and well are not essential. You can omit the summer sail and rudder as well. Steering is done with an oar by all web-footed baymen. There's a trick to this. Kneeling on the floor, put an oar over the lee side and scull her head around until the sail fills. As she gains way, the tendency of the oar is to come out of water. To prevent this, turn the blade from a vertical position through about 30°. The forward motion of the boat will then keep the oar under water. You must learn to do this with one hand because you will need the other to tend sheet. Or you may wish to use Wigeon as an all-purpose boat that you will share with your family, and then you will shoot the works and build with all appurtenances.

The sneakbox is a safe and seaworthy boat for children learning to sail. Witness the hundreds of one-design Perrines, named after their builder, Samuel Perrine of Barnegat, New Jersey. Many of today's top skippers learned the rudiments of racing in these little sneakboxes. The lateen rigs of the Sunfish and Sailfish (which accomplish the same thing) were not common when we designed the boat, but several builders of this boat recently used the readily available Sunfish/Sailfish sails with excellent results.

If you decide to install a centerboard, which is essential if you want to sail her, refer to the detail drawing on the plan and build the well before you put on the forward deck. Cut a ¾-inch slot in the center of the keel and carefully fit the head ledges, making the mortised end extend through the keel to be sawed off flush with the bottom. Ribs and gussets at stations 7 and 8 must be cut through to take bed logs.

The well cap extends from station 7 to 9 flush with the deck frames. It is ¾ × 3⅝-inch pine, and here again head ledges are mortised into it. Frame 8 should not be placed until the well cap is in and then is cut and mortised to it. The well slot through the cap is 1½ inches wide to permit the ⅜-inch plywood sides of the well to come through and butt against the deck. Start the well from the bottom, planing the bed logs to conform exactly to the curve of the keel. Rabbet their upper edge to receive the ⅜-inch plywood sides, which are carried up through the cap.

Use plenty of soft-setting marine glue where bed logs meet the keel and on other parts of the well. Secure bed logs to keel with 2-inch No. 10 screws on 3-inch centers. Paint the inside of the well as it is constructed. Before decking, install the mast step partner, which is flush with the top of the frames, install reinforcing blocks under the oarlocks, and bolt on the outboard bracket. If you use the sail only, attach a 1 × 1-inch rise to carry lag screws to hang the rudder. If you plan to use both motor and sail, make a detachable oak outboard bracket slightly tapered to drop into metal channels and forked to slip over the rudder riser. Just above the fork, insert a ¼-inch galvanized bolt on either side of the bracket.

Bow and stern decks are ¼-inch plywood and, after careful fitting, are glued and screwed to the side planks on 2-inch centers and to frames on 6-inch centers, all with ¾-inch No. 6 screws.

Next install coaming around the cockpit, oarlocks, ½-inch quarter-round trim around the coaming, 1-inch half-round rail, 1-inch half-round gunwale, brackets and cleats for the decoy rack, skeg, and, of course, the spray curtain.

Usually sneakbox oarlocks are made to fold down against the deck to get them out of sight. The inboard bottom side of the oarlock block is quarter-rounded so that it will fold inboard. The fit must be so close that the upright block jams slightly inside the vertical position and is held there by a small chock wedged into a deck cleat and a notch in the oarlock itself. Folding oarlocks are not too important. They may be solidly bolted to the deck if preferred.

The decoy rack should need no explanation. It is made of ½ × 6-inch siding. Two cleats on the stern portion fit into sockets fastened to the stern transom. At the forward end the sides fit behind the oarlocks, and near the stern, they engage the end of a cleat on each side. Finally hooks and eyes fasten them to the stern piece.

The rack is the handiest method of stacking decoys I know. It will accommodate thirty to forty stools, sloped on their tails. If anchors are dropped from side to side in regular order, the decoys may be put out without fouling anchors or lines, provided you unload them in the reverse order.

The three deck frames (4, 5, and 6) cut out to make the cockpit are used to frame a hatch. Cut two hatch ends ½ × 2 inches to fit the outside of the coaming ends and on the same curve. Temporarily fasten these in place and spring two pieces, ½ × 2 inches, around the cockpit side and fasten them to the hatch ends. Next notch the saved pieces of the deck frames (4, 5, and 6) halfway through to fit over the coaming, and glue and screw them to the hatch sides at intervals. Over all, glue and screw a piece of ¼-inch plywood to complete the hatch. At the stern end of the underside of the finished hatch, fasten a Z-shaped metal bracket that will slide snugly under the deck. At the bow, fasten a hasp with staple on the deck so that a padlock will protect your gear stowed inside. The hatch is left ashore when afloat.

The midships section shows ½ × 6-inch shelves on both sides extending from stations 4 to 6. These are not essential but are very handy to store shells, lunch, duck calls, and other small gear.

Of vital importance to the hunter going to windward in cold weather is the spray curtain. With this gadget, your sneakbox will shed water like a duck. Heavy seas rolling over the bow will part on the curtain and wash to either side. Start with a 1-inch curtain pole, 18 inches long. With this held upright at the center of the coaming, measure the distance to the top of one oarlock and double this. You will need a piece of 10-ounce tan canvas approximately 3 × 7½ feet. Cut the long dimensions of the canvas exactly to your measured distance and sew a hem in one edge to take a ¼-inch cotton rope. At the center of the hem sew a 3-inch triangular gusset and next to the hem place a grommet that takes the pointed end of the curtain pole. Put brass screw eyes at the oarlock corners and fasten the rope ends to them. With the pole in place, draw the center of the canvas taut to a point a few inches aft of the mast hole. Turn the canvas under and fasten to the deck. With surplus material turned under all around, tack to deck on curve, as shown on the plan, and also down the side of the oarlock. When completed, cut off surplus material from the inside.

Here a word about propelling the boat with oars. They should be stout 7-foot ash. Baymen always row a sneakbox seated on the floor so that when the curtain is up no spray bothers them. When pursuing crippled ducks, if it is not blowing too hard, face the bow while kneeling at the stern and push the boat forward with the oars while keeping the swimming duck continuously under observation.

If you build with a centerboard well, you will find a "jab board" a great convenience. It is simply a 1 × 6-inch board, 7 feet long, pointed on one end, with a cleat at the other end to serve as a handhold, that is thrust down the well into the bottom of the bay to hold the boat when setting out decoys.

Gunning Johnboat

This is the classic duckboat. Flat-bottom construction, sled bow, curved deck, and general construction methods give all you need to revamp to suit your own requirements. This little boat was designed for pond work, but you can enlarge as you see fit, beefing up specifications as you increase in size. You want to come in around 12 to 13 feet for a one-man boat, 14 or 15 feet for a two-man. If you prefer a sharp bow, which is slightly more seaworthy though it extends length without adding usable space, redraw the bow to bring the planks together and back with a stem piece as used in the scullboat plans.

Every duck hunter has his own ideas about a boat, so you'll probably redraw her. My only admonition is that if you do, I'd suggest you loft her final lines full size on paper as described. An additional virtue of this boat, besides all its virtues as the perfect duckboat, is that it will plane with fairly little power. If you make her large, say 14 feet, and wish to use a 10- to 20-hp engine, you'll have to beef her up considerably with heavier planking and transom knees. The flat-bottomed shape is the simplest of all to build, and with any carpentry skill at all, you should be able to produce the boat of your dreams. As designed, she is a boat for the ponds. Weight is about 80 pounds, and with a maximum width of 44 inches, she slides inside a standard station wagon's usual 45-inch horizontal clearance. If you drive a minicar, she'll ride on top in high style.

Best of all, she employs the classic johnboat shape that is the simplest, cheapest, and quickest to build. Since today you can tape the seams and thus avoid the necessity of making a true watertight connection, I wouldn't hesitate to say that if you can pound a nail into a board, saw a straight line, and read a ruler, you can put this boat together. I think the cost would be about $250.

There are some exciting features about her that aren't readily apparent. Waterline beam at 38 inches is a nice compromise. It floats the boat in around 5 or 6 inches of water with you in it, which is important in so many ducking spots where the water gets thin, yet the beam is enough to handle the power of a small outboard. A 3-hp would be about tops and the little 1½-hp is perfect and light as a feather. I'm stressing lightness here because this is the kind of boat you drag across a field or a marsh. For that, you need a flat bottom and a weight of less than 100 pounds. I'd guess speed at 3 or 4 mph with the 1½ hp, maybe 5 or 6 with the 3 hp.

This boat's virtue is her small size. She isn't made for doing any rough-water work, though her deck and spray shield will help if you do have to come home against a bad blow. The sled bow will make her throw water like a firehose, but you can sit on the floor to keep her center of gravity low and hide behind the spray shield. If you are running in a following sea, sit on the floor and lean back against the after coaming so your back and arms will help turn any waves that want to join the party. It's better not to put her to any such tests, however, but to use her in sheltered bays, rivers, and ponds.

This little rascal will row. The rocker (curve) in her bottom and toward the stern helps that, but with no roundness to her bottom and her short length, she'll be cranky—okay for picking up decoys but not so hot for chasing down cripples. The motor would be a wise partner for her.

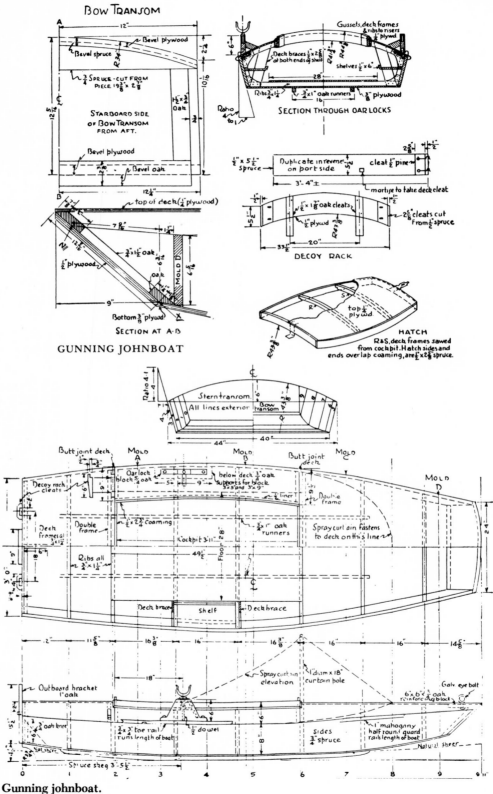

BOW TRANSOM

STARBOARD SIDE of BOW TRANSOM FROM AFT.

SECTION THROUGH OAR LOCKS

DECOY RACK

HATCH

R&S. deck frames sawed from cockpit. Hatch sides and ends overlap coaming, are ½"x2⅝ spruce.

SECTION AT A·B

GUNNING JOHNBOAT

Gunning johnboat.

BUILDING THE JOHNBOAT. You set this boat up with forms that you throw away, except for the transom. First lay out two straight, sturdy stringers, block them at right angles, and brace them with 2-by-4s. Lay out the molds with great care. It's best to draw them on construction paper and use these as templates. Draw the lines on ⅝-inch plywood to avoid warping and saw carefully. Notch each mold to take a ¾-inch-square gunwale and chine (bottom) batten. Don't notch the transom for these, however. Screw a block on the transom and screw the batten ends to it. (You'll throw these battens away. They are used only to scribe the gunwale and chine lines to the sides.) This gives the boat her pleasing shape and sheer (curve). Molds attach to stringers upside down. You build the bottom first, then turn her over. Transom arcs (the round tops of bow and stern) extend over stringers at either end.

The transom should be cut from ½-inch plywood. The arc for it and the deck

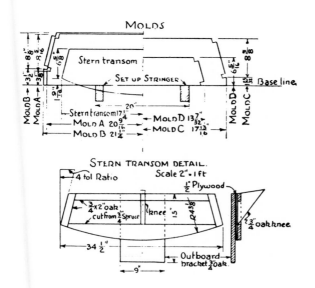

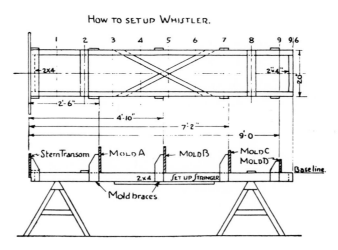

Gunning johnboat

beams is from a circle with a radius of 43⅛ inches. Cut the sides using the 4:1 ratio (or taking measurements off the scaled plans). Then screw ¾ × 2-inch oak or mahogany pads along bottom and sides as shown in the drawings. Fasten the transom temporarily on the stringers, like the molds, placing them carefully at right angles.

The sides are made from ¾-inch spruce or cedar, two planks 10 feet long, 12 inches wide. Clamp the planks to the transom at the stern, then make a Spanish rope windlass at the bow to draw the planks in. Soaking the planks will make them bend more easily. This, incidentally, is a compound curve, and plywood won't bend to it. Be careful so you don't pull the molds out of true. With the planks flat, scribe the side contours from the previously laid battens. Saw planks to shape, leaving an extra ¼ inch for planing true (fairing). Shape the bow according to "Section at A-B," locate points X and Z, and saw sides to this line. Both sides should be identical. Place a straightedge across the ends and plane them fair to receive bow transom.

Bow transom is ½-inch plywood. Draw it directly from the boat, not the lines, to compensate for any errors. Cut it slightly larger than the distance between the sides and about 15 inches top to bottom. Draw the arc at top to a 34-inch radius. Deck arc is 43⅛ inches, but pitching the bow forward requires a different curvature for bow transom. Temporarily fasten to sides (transom overlaps them), scribe, and cut to fit. Leave about ⅛ inch extra at top to plane flat to receive the deck. Remove bow transom and screw-glue oak or mahogany pads as shown, then screw-glue bow transom to sides. Now go to the stern, unclamp stern transom, and screw-glue it to sides.

Turn the hull over and plane the sides flat to receive the flat bottom. Remove the chine batten. You are ready to frame. Make frames (ribs) of light cedar or spruce. Nail or screw and glue, using ¼-inch plywood gussets on one side only. (You don't need double gussets.) You'll have to plane the ribs at top and bottom to compensate for the side angle. Don't forget to put limber holes in the bottom ribs.

You can use ⅜-inch plywood for the bottom, as called for in the original design, but I would prefer to use ¼-inch and glass it. My pondbox is ¼-inch throughout and has served for five seasons and is still in good shape, despite hard use and no care. I did punch a hole in the bow, but this boat is not fully glassed; only the seams are taped for waterproofing. If it were covered with lightweight glass or Dynel, it would be much stronger.

Temporarily fasten the bottom sheet to the sides, scribe the shape, remove, and saw. Fasten with glue and nails on 2-inch centers on the side and 6-inch centers into the frames.

Unscrew molds from stringers and turn the boat over. Fair sides level with gunwale batten, then remove the batten and all the molds. Saw out the nine deck frames to the 43⅛-inch radius, as described. They'll cut out of a ¾-inch plank 1½ inches thick. Use spruce or cedar. Double the frames at cockpit ends and where the side deck next to the cockpit is installed. Screw-glue arcs at transom tops. Leave frames across cockpit uncut until you install deck braces, then fair all surfaces with a plane, using a long straightedge so that all surfaces butt neatly, and sides are angled to take deck. Put in the oak knee at transom. Cut the cockpit frames and install cockpit liner. Save frames cut away to use for building hatch. Fasten ½ × 2¼-inch coaming to cockpit liners.

Here I am in the Zackbox, pondbox in tow.

The deck goes on in four pieces. Temporarily screw deck panels in place, scribe, re-move, and cut. Glue and nail deck beams on 2-inch centers on sides, 6-inch centers on deck frames. Put a 1-inch rub rail at gunwale. Plans show a galvanized eyebolt at deck top, but the boat will tow and come up a trailer more easily if you install it low just above the waterline on the bow. Plans show oak runners on the bottom. If you will be dragging the boat much, don't install these or skeg. Keep skeg, though, if you can since it will make the boat track better towing or rowed. Cockpit floor is ¼-inch, but you had better double-support it where you step in the boat. Don't extend it beyond where you sit.

The rest is incidental. The hatch is easily fashioned using the sawed frames of the cockpit. Build up oarlocks as shown. Add decoy racks if desired. (I find them handy to store blocks temporarily when putting out or picking up decoys.) Oars should be 7-footers. Cut the spray canvas and tack to the deck. Sew in the pocket or install a grommet at the top to hold it erect on the stick. I found that with shock cord I could hold almost all decoys inside a cup made from the spray shield. This little shelf inside is indispensable for holding shells, calls, hip flask, *Know Your Ducks*, etc. I couldn't keep the bottom of my sneakbox dry (tracking in water and mud getting in and out) and my regular canvas bag in which I kept my essentials got so cruddy that I made a special plywood box to fit under the transom. Now my gear stays clean and dry. The hatch is important because you can leave the boat in the rain without its filling and, of course, it locks. Note the hatch device that slides under the deck. Make it from bar aluminum if you can't find brass.

Pondbox

I built this box when I switched from gunning big water to gunning a little pond. I thought I'd use the boat to set out and pick up decoys and do my gunning out of the sinkbox. After bailing out the box several times, I dug a slot for the boat and gunned out of it if I was alone.

It is a minimal vessel, I'll admit, but it's easy and cheap to build, safely stable, doesn't row as badly as you'd expect, tows okay, and is warm and comfortable to gun from. You could make it strong enough to take a small motor, but you'd have to beef it up considerably from what I'll describe.

MATERIALS. The boat is designed to utilize 10-foot sections of exterior-grade ¼-inch plywood, which is easily obtainable. You'll need three sheets. One sheet builds the top and one side; another builds the bottom and the other side; the last builds the ends and hatch cover and provides scrap for gussets and supports. The carlings must be sawed. Use ½-inch stock. Good clear pine is okay, but oak or mahogany is better. All junctures are butted with ¾-inch-square molding strips. Glue with Weldwood and nail with ¾-inch galvanized nails to hold until the glue dries. A saber saw, plane, hammer, and backing weight, some glass tape and resin, and a pot of duckboat paint complete the required materials. You'll have change from $150 even after you buy oars and a preserver cushion.

DESIGN. Don't make the cockpit smaller than 24 inches wide and 30 inches long or it will be clumsy to get into and out of. You want an afterdeck to position your weight amidships, so the bow doesn't hunker up when you lean back in the water. Stability at 36-inch beam is okay. You can stand up in her. She'll be cranky to row, especially without an exterior keel. Leaving it off makes it easy to drag in and out of grass. Floorboards aren't needed, since you sit on a preserver cushion. The cover makes it possible to lock the boat with hasps at both ends. You can build decoy racks at either end or, as I do, store the blocks inside her.

POND BOX

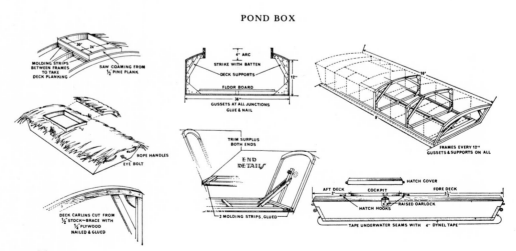

Pond box.

The coffinbox is a stripped-down pondbox built in my patented can't-go-wrong method. Each section is added as you go along. First cut out bottom.

BUILDING THE PONDBOX. Use my can't-go-wrong building method developed at great expense over the years. Start with the bottom. Cut one sheet to 36 inches, then take 12 inches off one end to provide for the bow and transom angle. Nail and glue the chine strips (of ¾-inch-square stock) ¼ inch in from either side. The side planking is set on the bottom in this boat. Nail and glue crossribs or frames from side to side on about 12-inch centers. Put the keel of the same ¾-inch stock on the inside or outside, whichever you prefer. Take two sections of the ¾-inch stock and glue them together. Then glue them in position at bow and stern with enough sticking out so that you can plane in the angle. This part of the job, including building the hatch, can be done in a shop since everything can be carried through a door.

Put the bottom on horses and cut the sides. Nail and glue to chine strip. Extend the frames up the sides and at each junction glue and nail a gusset to strengthen the joint. Leave room for the carlings.

The deck carlings and the hatch coaming must be sawed. Take a pliable batten and strike a 4-inch arc. Get 1½-inch clear pine in 8-inch or 10-inch planks. You can saw several frames out of one spot then. Because pine isn't strong, I braced mine with plywood carlings nailed and glued to the pine. I can sit on the deck without worrying. Cut the hatch coaming from the ½-inch carling at each end so it stands up enough to receive the sides of the hatch above the deck. Cut the sides of the hatch to fit over it generously because it will swell. Saw a couple of carlings to strengthen the hatch.

Plank the hatch cover. Plywood will bend one way but not the other. I learned this the hard way, even jacking a clamp right through the wood. If you get the right bend, it can be made to bend fairly easily. Put the carlings in the hatch cover after you glue and nail it to the ends.

The deck carlings sit on the ends of the side frames. Remember, you left space for them there. Gusset each at the joint. Then cut plywood strips about 2½ by 12 inches and nail and glue two supports at each carling. Make sure you cut them so that the nonbendable way functions to support. They will make the deck strong. The carling must be angled at either end to the angle of the transom, and the bow will have to be built slightly oversize. This way you can rasp the surplus away so it will receive the deck. (I forgot this and had to fill the void with a mixture of Weldwood glue and sawdust.) You can attach these carlings when you plank the ends.

Turn the boat over and plane the bow and transom angles into the two endpieces that you glued together. Fit the end planking, fiddling with it until you get a good fit.

Here's how the chine strips are put on. Butter the facing sides with Weldwood glue. Fasten with galvanized nails to hold until the glue sets up. Use a backing hammer to draw nails tight.

You can see how the box takes shape. Dots are ribs that run up either side and meet deck carlings on top. If you plan to dig the box in earth, make it as narrow as is comfortable. If you float her, expand beam out to 30 inches or so.

Run a piece of the ¾-inch-square stock up the middle of the endpieces and out along the bottom. Glue gusset supports to it so the through bolt for towing is strong. Use a ¼-inch galvanized eyebolt for this. While you're drilling for these, drill two holes for rope handles. Knot ¼-inch nylon line between the holes to make handling the boat easier.

Turn the boat back over and glue and fit the carlings at transom and bow end. Cut the deck so the bendable way is from side to side. The deck is fastened with the same screws as the boat; galvanized is fine. The screws make it possible to remove the deck if you ever have to make repairs. Get the deck with the bendable way right and screw down the centerline on each carling and thereafter at 6-inch intervals toward the bow. The plywood will lie down that way without clamps.

Once the deck is planked, turn the boat bottom up and round the plywood edges with a rasp. Fill all voids with a mixture of glue and sawdust or plastic putty.

The oarlocks have been raised to row. Rig locks that fold down like those on a plywood sneakbox or bolt pieces to the side and mount a galvanized lock to take them.

It may look awful, but it works fine. The boat is cranky and horrible to row, probably the worst I've ever experienced, but it doesn't have to go far.

Paint the boat outside and inside where you can reach with duckboat brown paint. Grass it up and she's ready to go. If you build and use one, drop me a note and tell me about it. If you're not pleased with it, I'll eat a seagull.

Completed box without deck looks like this. Dig this down 6 inches and it disappears. Box is warm and cozy to gun from.

This is a high-speed Air Gator airboat that costs over $6,000 but exceeds 60 mph. A super machine.

Airboats

Any hunting or fishing area that is plagued with shallow water is an automatic candidate for an airboat. Likewise rocky rivers. Centers for airboats that I know of are Florida, the Gulf Coast, and the Susquehanna River. Airboats vary from the very crude ones that need an inch or two of water at all times to high-speed ones that will climb right up a dryland dike.

One problem with airboats is that companies who make them keep going out of business. Air Gator and Susquehanna Air Motor are all on again, off again, and their status at any given time is at best hazy. At this writing, Air Cat, P.O. Box 8, Lake Hamilton, FL 33851 (813-439-1152), is advertising its Tomcat, powered by a VW engine, at $2,800. They build fifteen models, from the Tomcat to a big 17-footer with 100 pound-plus payloads. Their catalogue costs $2.

One firm that has stood the test of time is Banks–Maxwell, and it is perfectly suited to this book. Although its boats are not the 100-mph speedsters of southern Florida, Banks–Maxwell tailors its sales toward the backyard home builder. Hulls are standard aluminum johnboat hulls, and kit hulls of plywood are offered. Banks–Maxwell supplies the airboat parts and full instructions in their use. They supply mount parts and directions on how to rig them, a variety of prop choices, and a variety of engine choices using Franklin and Continental aircraft engines as well as Volkswagen and Corvair air-cooled auto conversions. Anyone interested in airboats should have a current copy of their catalogue. Send $1 to Macon Banks, Banks–Maxwell, P.O. Box 3301, Ft. Worth, TX 76105; or phone 817-535-3698.

This is the kind of boat you get if you build up from Banks-Maxwell components. No great speed but excellent shallow-water capability.

Barge Blinds

The barge blind is an entirely new concept in duckboats. Nothing like it ever existed before. The boat was designed and the plans were drawn by Bill Phillips.

If you build a 14-foot plywood barge from the plans and fiberglass it for strength, ice protection, and watertight integrity, it will cost about $500 if you don't make any expensive errors. The cost in time is also immense — eighty hours or so.

The best way to build a barge blind is to use an aluminum johnboat hull. Look at the advantages. Aluminum requires no maintenance and will last years longer than the plywood. It is impervious to rot. It is stronger than plywood and lighter by at least 150 pounds. One 17-foot, three-man, plywood barge actually tipped a scale at 600 pounds. An aluminum one will weigh around 160 pounds. A Monark 16-foot, especially roomy, *commercial* boat weighs 280. Which one would you like to winch up a steep ramp?

However, none of these reasons is as significant in my view as the fact that if you buy a commercial model you will get a balanced and graceful hull that will outperform practically any hull you can make out of plywood. In the Monark MV series (more to come) you get a tough rough-weather boat, a real performer that can handle horsepower.

A lot of companies build johnboats — Polar Kraft, Delhi, Sears, Appleby, Smokercraft. None has as many different models as Monark. For example, Ouachita offers eleven different models. These vary in size, hull thickness, and beam. I had a Ouachita johnboat, and it was a neat little boat. (Somebody tried to steal it, too.)

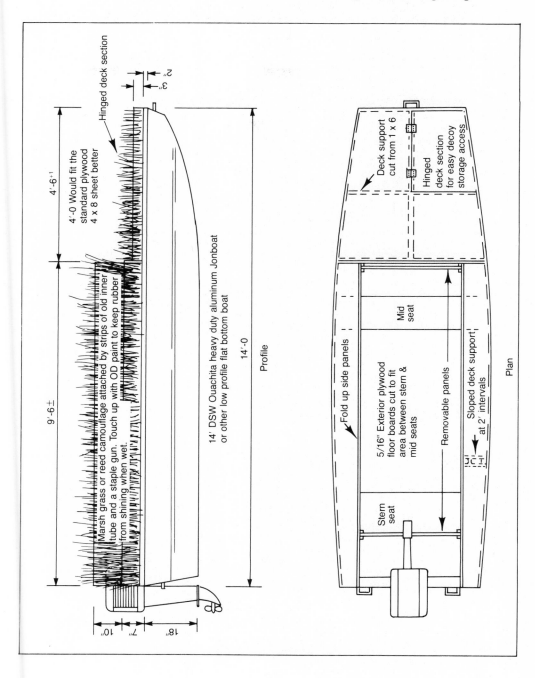

Hinged deck section

4'-0 Would fit the standard plywood 4 x 8 sheet better

4'-6'⁺¹

9'-6'±

2"

3"

Marsh grass or reed camouflage attached by strips of old inner tube and a staple gun. Touch up with OD paint to keep rubber from shining when wet.

14' DSW Ouachita heavy duty aluminum Jonboat or other low profile flat bottom boat

14'-0

Profile

10"

7"

18"

Deck support cut from 1 x 6

Hinged deck section for easy decoy storage access

Fold up side panels

5/16" Exterior plywood floor boards cut to fit area between stern & mid seats

Mid seat

Removable panels

Sloped deck support at 2' intervals

Stern seat

Plan

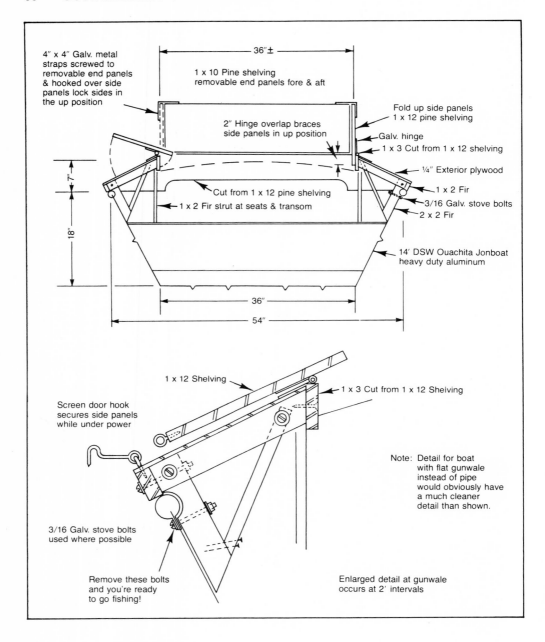

4" x 4" Galv. metal
straps screwed to
removable end panels
& hooked over side
panels lock sides in
the up position

36"±

1 x 10 Pine shelving
removable end panels fore & aft

2" Hinge overlap braces
side panels in up position

Fold up side panels
1 x 12 pine shelving

Galv. hinge
1 x 3 Cut from 1 x 12 shelving

¼" Exterior plywood

1 x 2 Fir

3/16 Galv. stove bolts

2 x 2 Fir

Cut from 1 x 12 pine shelving
1 x 2 Fir strut at seats & transom

14' DSW Ouachita Jonboat
heavy duty aluminum

7"

18"

36"

54"

1 x 12 Shelving

1 x 3 Cut from 1 x 12 Shelving

Screen door hook
secures side panels
while under power

Note: Detail for boat
with flat gunwale
instead of pipe
would obviously have
a much cleaner
detail than shown.

3/16 Galv. stove bolts
used where possible

Remove these bolts
and you're ready
to go fishing!

Enlarged detail at gunwale
occurs at 2' intervals

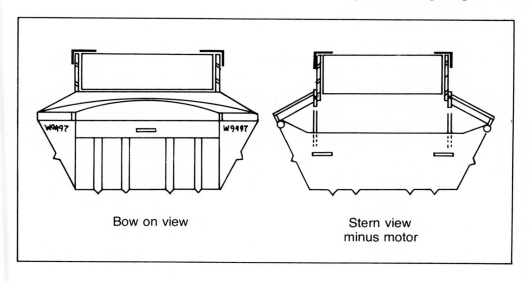

Bow on view

Stern view
minus motor

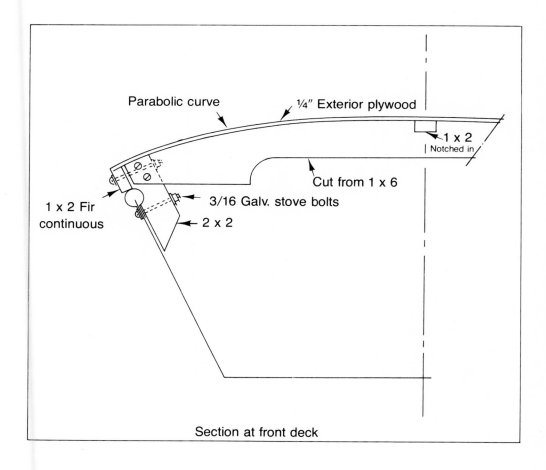

Parabolic curve

¼″ Exterior plywood

1 x 2
Notched in

Cut from 1 x 6

3/16 Galv. stove bolts

1 x 2 Fir
continuous

2 x 2

Section at front deck

By contrast, Monark has thirty-four models. They all vary according to beam and length, seat placement (which the catalogue shows), hull gauge, and bow shape. Monark's standard boats are .063-gauge aluminum. The company offers johnboats designed for heavy-duty commercial work with .072-gauge aluminum and heavier frames. These cost slightly more but would be absolute crackers for a barge. In addition, the Monark MV series takes the regular johnboat shape and puts a slight V in the forward hull and a V-shaped bow that turns rough water. I'll mention some specific boats, but suffice it to say that if there's a barge in your future, send for Monark's fine color catalogue at Monark Boat Co., Box 210, Monticello, AR 71655.

About a 36-inch beam at the bottom is the minimum beam that you'd want. I'd think the more beam you could get, the better it would be. The boat would tip less with two men sitting with the weight mostly on one side. Beam on barges of the guy who invented them was always at least 60 inches, and 72 in the latest models.

After you select your hull, what you do next is a little designing. If I know duck hunters, everybody will have his own idea about how to finish the boat. Basically what you want to do is put on a foredeck extending from the bow up to and including the first seat. This deck then extends down the side to the transom. To it are hinged panels on either side that fold up to form the front and back of the blind. Deck and panels are grassed. When the panels are in place, two more panels are slipped in sideways at the transom and the end of the front deck. These keep birds that are circling the bow or stern from spotting you. Both men are warm and cozy—completely protected, down in the boat out of the wind. The bow man sits right behind the second seat, stern man at the rear of the boat. There is a seat separating the two, which is

Bill Phillips' completed barge looks like this. A neat, trailerable, duck-killing machine.

This is what a layout boat looks like. The curved section lies flat in the water. The man lies in a box about 6 inches deep that is submerged.

handy for shells, calls, thermos, lunch, and your retriever to repeatedly sweep into the bilge with his tail.

To keep down slop, put down floorboards. (Duckboats have more ways to get water in them. The retriever alone coming aboard brings in a gallon.) Hunters sit on life-preserver cushions. The total weight of the blind will be about 85 pounds.

Layout Boats

Gunning ducks from open water is one of waterfowling's deadliest techniques. The reason is simple: Almost all the danger ducks face comes from land. Water areas far from shore are sanctuaries; they represent safety. Hence open-water birds are less wary, decoy more readily, and use less frequently that maddening diver trait of sitting down on the far edge of the spread.

Trouble is there aren't many good layout boats available. You can—as plenty do—gun out of barge-blind boats. But these have such a high profile even when grassed up that they spell danger to wary species like the mallards and pintails. Even the divers will often shy from them in all but bad weather. They work best in areas where they blend with bank or grass clumps.

The finest open-water rig ever devised was the sinkbox of old. This was a coffinlike box, just big enough to hold a man lying down. To keep the box stable, large flat decks extended in all directions. Any waves would break on these decks and not in the box. To adjust for the weights of different gunners, iron decoys were spread out on the decks, and, of course, these added to the decoy appeal. With the man lying prone, the box was all but invisible and the ducks were at the gunner's mercy. The sinkbox was deadly and was quite properly outlawed years ago.

An enterprising Detroit River, Michigan, guide named Hy Dahlka went back to the sinkbox for inspiration and came up with a design that has to be the finest open-water boat being used today. The gunner lies in an underwater slot that allows the boat to sink the maximum amount with the least weight. Yet to keep both game warden and the waves at bay, a rounded, curved deck extends above the waves. The flat section of the upper hull makes the vessel extremely stable in the water. This is important because it provides a more stable shooting station. (I shot sea ducks last season out of a rocking boat, and it was nearly impossible to hit them.) Also it will make a much less tipsy platform for getting in and out of the boat when gunners change.

Obviously a boat designed to be as low to the water as possible isn't going to be too heroic at keeping the water out if it gets rough. Anti–wave-slop insurance is provided by an ingenious canvas-and-aluminum-pipe spray shield. This adds height to the profile, but the increased waves are at the same time decreasing the visibility. In calm weather, the shield is left down.

But a layout rig does have some disadvantages. The boat is anchored on station and stays there. Since it can't be rowed or paddled, a tender is required both to transport the vessel to the shooting ground and to retrieve downed birds. Conceivably you could rig a spot for a retriever, but on big, open water that isn't altogether safe for the retriever. Obviously, someone has to man the tender, and that means that he is watching rather than gunning. And there is real danger in this rig. You are helpless in the boat. I would suggest that a thick flotation parka be added to the legal requirement for a PFD. Experienced layout gunners advise that a 24 × 24-inch fluorescent flag on a 3-foot staff be another requirement for signaling not only to your own tender in case of emergency but also to oncoming craft that might run the boat down before it was sighted. And some provision should be added for breakdown of the tender. I'd want a walkie-talkie in contact with a shore station.

There are several advantages of a layout rig. One of the most obvious is mobility: You can gun waters the birds are using. No permissions are needed. You can load and launch at public ramps. The boat can easily be expanded to accommodate two hunters. The tender needs no camouflage because it sits on station. Positioned a couple of hundred yards downwind, the ducks will ignore it. Any summer runabout will do nicely without modification other than a rigging place to transport the layout boat. And if that becomes a problem, the layout can be cartopped easily.

On open water under most circumstances it would be hard to get puddle ducks to come to this rig. Add some wind and snow or ice and you have another story. You could expect some to come to you, especially juveniles. And in areas where you could get some concealment around the vessel — among islands, in grass or brush — you could fool the best of them. In the midwest where more and more duck shooting is taking place in fields, the boat could easily be dug into the ground and thereby offer both concealment and warmth.

If you're courageous you can build from my crude drawings here. Serious builders should send for really detailed plans and building instructions. Send $8 to Mr. Teri Klein, P.O. Box 8365, Erie, PA 16505. He also builds a few boats in fiberglass and will submit prices on request.

10
Houseboats

The world has definitely progressed backward where houseboats are concerned. Years back, waters were dotted with them. They'd do ducking duty on the marshes fall and winter. In the spring they'd move behind the inlets where the big weakfish and stripers lurked. And it's so great to be living afloat. And to be in the duck marshes at night, all night. You hear the birds calling and winging overhead. The activity at night can give you a good clue as to why the birds tend to sit tight and disappear during the day.

At one time I knew some fellows who tucked a little houseboat in the marsh before every season. I watched the boat being moored closer and closer to the marina. Then finally one season the boat stayed ashore where they could get water and electric power. I guess that's what did houseboats in. Too much trouble tending to them. Too much risk of damage or loss when savage winter storms rage.

Yet it shouldn't be. Now, with modern houseboats so much better than wooden versions of yesteryear, there ought to be more guys using them as hunting and fishing headquarters. With fiberglass you don't have to worry about ice pulling out the caulking or damaging the hull or the doggone boat springing a leak. Previously, heating and light depended on kerosene — smelly and somewhat dangerous stuff. Now the RV people have solved household problems with propane. Heaters are near-instantaneous and absolutely safe. Stoves turn on at the flick of a wrist. Propane lights are soft and subtle. There is even a tasteless antifreeze on the market that you can add to your water tank so there's not even any need to drain the tank when you leave the boat. A CB radio keeps you in touch no matter how remote you locate the boat.

There are admitted disadvantages to a houseboat, of course. You can't put any boat aside and forget about it. Houseboats require care on a fairly frequent basis. The aforementioned storm risk is real, especially with the super snows and ice jams we're experiencing. Conditions are always crowded on a boat, and the heavy, usually muddy, ducking gear doesn't help.

Of course, if you get the houseboat notion, you can go out and buy one. They are the cheapest big boat you can buy, about half to two-thirds the price of a comparable conventional yacht. But I think if I was going to houseboating, I'd poke around boat-yards until I found one in rough shape that I could buy for a song. I'd take the engine out — probably an inboard-outboard — and throw it away. You can tow. It's probably shot from electrolysis (which is why the guy is selling the boat) and will be a continual nuisance. I'd seal the stern opening and figure on towing the boat where I wanted with a runabout. A fairly small outboard can tow a fairly good-sized boat. I'd take my cheapy and renovate the interior, avoiding boat-supply houses and buying all needed gear through trailer outlets. I'd design the inside to suit my taste, and I'd insulate the heck out of it, again trailer-style.

I'd try to find a fiberglass boat, because the hull would probably still be in good shape. There were a few aluminum-hulled boats built, and this material too should withstand the years gracefully. Steel is something else again. Around salt water, steel will probably deteriorate, and in fresh water it will hold up only if it's been properly maintained. The trouble with most steel houseboats is that you can't really maintain them. There are too many nooks and crannies you can't get at. Steel does have one advantage — it's easy to bring in a welder and rebuild a fresh new hull at moderate cost.

I'd get the biggest surplus Danforth-type anchors I could carry from a surplus ship chandler and moor the boat with heavy nylon ropes to at least two of them — or better still to trees, if there are any of those around, or a marina in the proper place. And when I tied it up or found a place to anchor I'd do so visualizing the 80-mph winds

Tucked in a small creek near where I once used to hunt was this houseboat garvey. Guys would live on her for several days at a time.

that are sure to blow. If I could find a cozy nest I could drive to, so much the better. There I would live in my houseboat listening to Chopin on the stereo, contemplating all the fish I will catch or ducks I will shoot, the envy of all.

Cabin Johnboat

This boat is the ugly duckling of the boating world. Yet it is an ugly duckling that turns into a swan when you go into the cabin. Here you'll find honestly livable quarters that two husky people can occupy over an extended period. That's not the only time the swanlike beauty appears. When you look at the vessel's price tag you'll feel as warm and cozy as you will in her heated cabin on a chilly night. She's cheap. For years this kind of boat was always the least expensive and most livable design for the money. It still is.

I need a boat like this to take me to my duck blind before daybreak. Then I'll gun until midmorning, when things slow down. About this time, I'll want a second breakfast and I'll go back to the boat, cook up a storm, then stretch out for a snooze. About two or three p.m. I'll be back in the blind. If I feel like it and things look good, I'll pull her into a creek, anchor fore and aft, and spend the night.

There's a big striper run in the spring down my way. April is the time, and believe me it's cold out on the water in early spring. But it would be easy to last all day with a toasty cabin to duck in and out of. Hot coffee would be on the stove. I could fish off the stern and live aboard for days at a time if I felt like it and the action was hot.

You see what I'm getting at. There is a real need for a boat in which one or two persons can pot around and take the fun where they find it. If it has a modest price tag, so much the better.

In some areas this boat is called a *gunning garvey*. A garvey is like a johnboat with maybe a little more grace. Yet it's basically a wall-sided, flat-bottom vessel with a sled bow and is the cheapest kind of vessel to build. Along the Mississippi and the southern waterways of the country this boat is called a *cabin johnboat*.

With all the emphasis on houseboats today, I've renamed the boat a *sportsman's houseboat*. So many small "yachts" offered today are more toy than boat. You might be able to spend a night in them, but to live in any comfort for any length of time, forget it. That isn't true of the houseboats. The square trailerlike form of this vessel permits adequate layout for living.

You can't buy this boat today as she sits. The boats that come closest to it are the cabin johnboats offered by Monark, Box 210, Monticello, AR 71655; or Smokercraft, New Paris, IN 46553. The 20-foot hulls sell for around $1,800. Smokercraft has a 24-foot so-called whitewater hull (the bow is raised, giving it a classy look) at 24-feet that would be a honey for this boat. Price is around $2,000. You could probably (maybe?) special order a boat without seats, lowering the costs slightly.

The big johnboat hulls are rated for big outboards, but you wouldn't need that to attain okay performance. The 18-foot aluminum cabin johnboat has been clocked at 22.7 mph driven by a Merc 35. A 50-hp motor drives her at 30.9 mph with four passengers. I'd expect this boat to plane with a 25-hp at 10-12 mph, reach 15-18 mph with a

33-hp, and hit 25 mph or more with a 50-hp. While the boat is clumsy-looking and will be subject to windage problems, the flat johnboat hull is stable and the weight of the cabin will sink the hull only an inch or two, thanks to its weight-carrying ability.

There must be no skimping on the size of things if you are to be comfortable aboard a boat. A seat less than 15 inches high will cramp your legs after a while. A bunk should be at least 24 inches wide and 6 feet 3 inches long — 6 feet 5 inches is better — or you won't rest easy. This boat has what is called sitting headroom — things are arranged in the cabin so you can cook, wash, and so on from a sitting position. Yet with almost 5 feet of headroom, you don't have to crawl on your knees to get around.

The sportsman's houseboat is what the name implies. It has no frills, no fancy stuff. But it is comfortable and livable over long periods and in all weather. Maintenance is minimum. Enjoyment is maximum. For a headquarters out on a lonely lake or down a pretty river, a little boat like this would be hard to beat.

BUILDING THE CABIN JOHNBOAT. Until some manufacturer starts offering one of these boats in all-aluminum, the only way you can get one is to build it yourself. You could start with the hull and build the whole thing, but I think it's foolish. The cost of wood, fiberglass-covered (for ice), will be so close to the price of an aluminum hull that it amounts to working hours and hours for almost nothing. And you wind up with a hull material that isn't as good. I would buy an aluminum hull on special order. And I'd have it over 20 feet so I wouldn't have to worry about level flotation. Order it without seats but with a net deck. This is a forward deck that slopes toward the bow and contains scuppers (holes) to drain water over the side. This will be your forward deck. It will weigh about 450-475 pounds. Transom is 20 inches.

It would be preferable to build the boat with side decks. The beam of the stock boats (76 inches) doesn't permit this and still enable you to keep 28-inch bunks and enough space to make it comfortable to traverse the aisle between. If you were starting the boat from scratch you could give the hull more freeboard and slightly more beam and carry the sheer of the forward deck up higher. With side decks she'd be handsome. But the stock hull will more than suffice.

Bolt 2 × 2-inch fir stringers about 12 inches long to the hull sides between every frame and at each end of the cabin. Use ¼-inch or ³⁄₁₆-inch stainless-steel bolts and washers for this. Any other material will corrode the aluminum. Then add the uprights. You can make them straight, but angling them in improves appearance and robs no usable space. The uprights butt to the frames and are held securely with plywood gussets on each side. Temporarily fasten these with galvanized screws. When everything is fair, remove and glue.

The cabin carlings must be sawn if a pleasing curve is to be attained. Use ¾-inch spruce or sweet pine for this. Smooth and round the underneaths so it won't hurt so much when you hit your head on them. Bolt carlings to the ends of the uprights.

Plank the cabin sides and top with ⅜-inch exterior plywood. Screw and glue to uprights and carlings. Use 2 × 2-inch stock at corners. Cut windows. Build doors. No hatch is shown over the after cabin door since the full windshield prevents it. On reflection I think I'd use a piece of Plexiglas only in front of the wheel and make a 30- or 36-inch hatch over the door. This slides forward on rails and opens the whole cabin up. It would make a nice place to stand, leaning on the roof, thinking uplifting thoughts.

When the cabin is complete, fiberglass all edges.

CABIN SOLE. Most aluminum johnboat hulls are framed with 2 × 2-inch aluminum frames. They aren't pleasant to walk on but are tolerable in the cockpit. The cabin sole (floor) should be covered with plywood laid on these, not only for comfort but to keep things dry if any water gets in the boat.

FLOTATION. Johnboats are made with Styrofoam-block flotation under the seats. You can build flotation in under the bunks, then aft along the sides and transom to float the motor. Cabin sides might also hold foam slates. Have plenty of life-preserver cushions around. It wouldn't be a bad idea to build a watertight bulkhead at the end of the cabin as high as you'd care to step over. Bunks are plywood with 3-inch foam in vinyl covers.

DOORS AND WINDOWS. If you are going to use the boat in hot weather you want good-sized doors and windows. If you plan to use it in cold weather, cut down on size or storm-strip them. Actually, with today's trailer heaters, you could heat any cabin. I'd be inclined to make her as light and bright as I could. I'd heat her with the stove and a catalytic heater or two—no carbon-monoxide danger with catalytics.

HEAD. No problem with the head. You can use several kinds, including a bucket (always works). A Porta-Pottie is okay in restricted areas. If a marine head is used, remember to bolt it with stainless-steel bolts. Use neoprene seals to prevent weeping.

SINK, STOVE, ICE BOX. Any LP stove is great—inexpensive, safe, and plenty hot. Self-contained sinks are available. Water is such a convenience you shouldn't do without. I'd use a portable icebox on a platform high enough to drain over the side. They are so cheap and so good. A locker under the sink might work for this.

LIGHTING. Good LP lights are available through trailer-supply houses. Also there are many battery-powered lamps. If you plan to use an electric motor, your battery can probably handle cabin lighting demands supplemented by battery lamps. A flat battery isn't as much of a problem with an outboard that can be started manually.

CANVAS TOP. A canvas top for sun and/or rain protection turns the cockpit area into living space. Glass for large windows should be safety glass or Plexiglas for safety. The cockpit rail can be omitted if you don't mind the risk of falling overboard.

More Houseboats

If the houseboat bug bites you, investigate the kit-boat plans books. Glen L has a neat little 24-footer, for example. Pontoon houseboats are also neat because they are so stable. Glen L has a variety of versions with interesting interior options. If you start designing your own, the easy way is to get some graph paper and make each square equal to 1 foot.

11
Customizing a Fisherman

With some fishing-oriented boat companies you can order the customized fishing gadgets you need in the salesroom. The salesman will stand there with his checklist and all you have to do is nod when he reads off items like compass, CB radio, poling platform, and so forth. The good news is that the gear that you get will be good stuff and probably installed properly (they've had experience with it) and whatever tailoring is required will be handled professionally. The bad news is, of course, the bill. You'll be charged top dollar for every item since the boat company, the dealer, and the guy doing the actual work all take a cut. The other bad news is that you might just not get exactly what you want. It might be added that all boat dealers and companies are not all that sharp about installations they do not deal with all the time.

More probably when you go to buy a new boat the dealer or boat company won't even offer items specifically tailored to fishing. You'll get a fire extinguisher, compass, running lights, and that's it. The rest is up to you.

To start we have to go back to our basic premise—that you don't want to be dependent on the meager choices offered by your local, or not so local, boat dealer. Two dollars invested in mail-order catalogues open the whole world to you at discount prices.

Safety Gear

The first thing you want to insist on is a fuse panel. Many boat companies ignore them, and wiring up a rig without fuses is asking for trouble. Like your boat catching fire. Cost is negligible. The fuse panel enables you to run a regular 115-volt cable, such as is used for wiring houses, directly from the battery to the fuse panel. Then everything else comes off the panel.

The first customizing should be done on the wiring system. All the fastenings should be soldered. Melt resin solder into the wires at all connectors. More modern rigs use snap connectors. A trick I've used is to insulate and isolate them with gobs of silicone plastics. This keeps moisture out, adds to the permanency of the connection, and takes only moments to do.

The next item you want is a fire extinguisher. The dry-chemical extinguishers are okay. You should mount the extinguisher where it is instantly at hand because speed is of such importance in fires. Mount the extinguisher on a bulkhead, inside a locker, on a fishing locker door, under the console. An overlooked mounting spot is under a seat. Whatever you do, don't throw the thing in a locker and forget it.

The third safety item you want is life jackets. There are so many great flotation jackets around now that are approved by the Coast Guard that we should all be wearing a jacket at all times when we're on the water. If the boat is under 16 feet, buoyant cushions are legal and more acceptable because new level flotation keeps the boat under you. Also they are at hand and can be thrown. Beyond 16 feet, you need a jacket type. Adult kapok vests are the cheapest at about $8. The trouble I've found with all the fabric covered jackets is that they mildew in lockers and eventually look scruffy, although their flotation is unaffected. Slab PVC vests cost about twice as much, but they stow tighter, and vinyl cleaners can keep them respectable looking. Chances are about 100,000 to one that the only use you'll ever have for a jacket beyond complying with the law is using one for a temporary buoy, or trip line to anchor or to mark a good fishing spot.

The latest Coast Guard regulation is that day and nighttime signalling devices be carried on boats using salt waters or the Great Lakes. Boats under 16 feet must carry night signals (flares); boats over 16 feet must carry both day and night signals. Day signal is an orange flag and/or smoke flares. Dealers have good inexpensive packages.

Lights

If you are a fisherman you'll be doing a lot of night running. The considerations here are more legal than practical. Generally you can see a great deal more running completely blacked out, but in a lot of places the marine police will get after you for it. What you want to try to do is position lights so they won't shine in your eyes. Boats over 26 feet require separate port and starboard sidelights and a white light forward. Boats under 26 feet have a combination bow light usually mounted on the nose of the bow. Any light up there will cast a glow that will restrict vision. There are a couple of ways to beat it. One is to get an aluminum beer can, flatten it, and fashion it into a light deflector. Spray your side flat black, but leave the other side shiny. Another approach is to mount separate side lights in boats under 26 feet and no bow light. As far as I can determine, this is legal. Acceptable lights on small boats are the battery-operated types that clamp on with C-clamps. The trouble I've had with them is that they are too cheap and are hard to keep working, since they soon get corroded.

A stern light is an important consideration to a fisherman. It shouldn't be permanent. You don't want anything back there in the stern sticking up to foul a line. In smaller boats the C-clamp lights solve the problem. In one boat I used a battery-powered, white, 360-degree light that mounted on a pole with a permanent fixture well below the gunwale. When not in use the light stowed below the gunwale, too. On larger boats, you want a bayonet mount that plugs into a permanent fixture on the transom deck. The fixture is flush with the socket, all belowdecks. When the light on its pole is not in use, it is stowed. A cover seals off the hole in the flush mount, mostly for looks.

Interior lighting inside the boat is a plus if you plan to night-fish at all. A couple of dome lights mounted under the gunwale can cast a soft illumination so you can see enough to change lures, take a fish off the hook, and so forth. At the same time the domes can be mounted low enough so the light doesn't actually shine on the water, which in some cases will scare the fish. Another night-fishing trick is to carry a small flashlight, not necessarily a penlight, but one that takes a couple of C batteries. This is just the right size to hold in your mouth, which lets you point it where you want and hold it steady but leaves both hands free to work the lures or unhook a fish.

There are a lot of spotlights available. The ones that mount permanently but allow the light to be removed add to versatility. The new flashlights like Kell or Pro lights that are really machined instruments made for police are useful for boat work because they stand up to shocks and corrosion. The portable spots, many in shockproof or waterproof cases working off a dry-cell or hotshot battery, can be stowed in a locker, available to show up stumps, rocks, numbers when needed.

Compasses

There are any number of good compasses on the market, and generally speaking in a small boat you don't need an expensive one. Your navigation can't be very precise,

Everything is ready for action here. Bait is in bucket. More in the cooler. What isn't needed is the stern light waiting to foul a line.

probably, and you can't steer a small boat within about 10 to 15 points of a course. The compass is generally something to get you home in a fog. The compass should be mounted so it reads almost in line with the helmsman's view ahead. He should have only to lower his gaze slightly to read the dial. Mount the compass so that turning the steering wheel won't affect the reading. Mounting the compass too close to a working tachometer or radio will distort the reading. Keep at least a couple of feet distance between them.

Tachometer

Did you know that everything about your engine is better if it runs right up to its rated rpm? It will stay in tune better, run smoother at both high and low speeds, be the most economical, and wear out slower. All these are good enough reasons why you should spend the extra bucks for a tachometer in any but very small boats. Coupled with the compass, a tach becomes a navigation tool. Let's say you like a certain spot in Toledo Bend. You work it out and write it down — from dock at XX degrees at 2,100 rpm. After XX minutes come to new compass heading XX. Run 8 minutes at 3,000 rpm . . . and there you are. Without the compass-tach combination you are Visual Flight Rules only.

Gas Tanks

There have been some important changes in the materials allowed for construction of marine fuel tanks, and it's important to know about them. Tanks are now made out of terne-plate steel. This is light steel covered with a lead alloy and painted with red fire-retardant paint. The familiar 3-gallon and 6-gallon outboard gas tanks are made of this material. Also available are aluminized steel tanks. These are steel tanks coated with aluminum. Finally, only a few years ago, several aluminum alloys were okayed for marine tanks.

If you have permanent in-place fuel tanks, aluminum is what you want. Do not accept any kind of steel tank under any circumstances. Test the tank with a magnet if you have any doubts. Thousands of boats were built with sealed-in-place terne-plate steel tanks, and the Coast Guard recommended recently that they be taken out and visually inspected every year (a mammoth undertaking in many boats) because they are floating bombs. Water eventually corrodes pin holes in them: the next thing you've got is leakage and the potential for explosion.

As grim as the bill will be if you have a boat that has one of these tanks, I urge you to replace it. In console boats this may require cutting through the cockpit floor. Even at that, it's worth it to replace a steel tank with an aluminum one. They aren't all that expensive — about $175 for a 20-gallon tank. These tanks are okay for diesel fuel, too.

So many million 6-gallon outboard tanks have served so well for so long that they don't need any more praise from me. In the open, airy, portable environment of an outboard, they are fully satisfactory because they are being constantly, if unconsciously, inspected. When they get pinholes and seepage starts (which is inevitable

Two rod storage areas in this console fisherman. Teak racks are under gunwales on both sides. Rods also fit in the console holders. Note recessed holder in decks for trolling position. Other nice features are transom baitbox and coaming padding for fighting fish standing up. Two problems: The white light to right of wheel would blind you at night, and where's the compass?

in time), it is apparent to both eye and nose and the tank gets replaced, probably not because of the explosive danger but because the skipper is too cheap to waste fuel.

The 6-gallon portables make good auxiliary units if your permanent tank isn't adequate. If you use one with an auxiliary outboard, make sure you can pump fuel from your permanent tank into it if you break down far enough offshore so the 6 gallons isn't enough to bring you home. A little PAR hand pump with suitable piping is enough. If, as often happens, you wind up with outboards of different makes, you'll have to use Rube Goldberg connectors so that both kinds of fittings can be used. I recently saw a spout that could be attached to the tanks. If you've ever tried to pour from an outboard tank, you know how handy that item can be.

Rod Storage

One of the most essential items for a small fisherman is some sort of way to hold the rods, both for storage and for trolling. Trolling is a nonrespectable form of fishing in some quarters, but it is one of the best ways to find fish in a new lake. In salt water and for species like walleyes and muskies, trolling is a way of life.

Storing the rods where they are out of the way, can't be stepped on, and won't be beat up by vibration is essential. Bass boats, of course, utilize built-in boxes that can be locked. Boston Whaler has long offered a lockable box on the rail aft. The rods stick forward under the pipe railing. On console boats, holders made of suitably-sized white PVC pipe hold the rods upright along the sides of the console. The rods, mostly the reels, intrude into the passageway between console and sides, but not enough to cause concern. Fishing-oriented console manufacturers like Mako, Grady White, and HydraSport offer holders made of teak along the console sides.

In almost any small boat the only unobstructed area is along the sides. Here you can make holders in a variety of ways. I found clear plastic holders that combine a loop and an S. The butt of the rod goes in the loop, and the tips lie in the S. Two on either side can hold four rods. Many guys fashion mahogany and even plywood imitations of the fancy teak holders. If you are in a hurry, buy flat aluminum bar stock, bend it, and wrap it with cotton line or tape to protect against chafing. Again, white PVC pipe is available through plumbing-supply houses and could be cut to receive butts and tips. Looks salty. Whatever you do, always bolt the holders to the sides, except in a fiberglass boat in which you may want to glass them in place. If your boat has a cuddy, you may be able to rig storage in it and be able to lock up your gear. I couldn't rig a good way to hold rods in the little cuddy on the Wellcraft, but they rested okay in one of the abbreviated bunks with their tips poked into the rope locker.

If your boat sports a hard cabin top, the classic place for rod storage is right under the cabin top, hanging the rods on the same sort of holders that work on the sides of the consoles. Another excellent spot for rods in a larger boat is all the way forward over the usual V berths forward. The reels are all the way forward, which keeps them out of the sleepers' faces. Another place to store rods is standing against the wall of a head, especially if it's a roomy head. In all cases if you take the reels off and stow them in their reel bags (after spraying down with CRC, of course, and backing off the drags), they are more easily stowed and take up far less room. I just counted twenty-four surf, big-game, fly, spinning, popping, and bait-casting rods in my office. About seven are hung on the side of a cabinet, and the rest are strewn about. One has been outside leaning next to my door for a year. Why? It's a non-ferruled surf rod, and there's no place the thing will fit.

Rod Holders

If you never troll you'll have no need of rod holders that put the rods into fishing position. Most of us like to be geared for it anyway just in case the spirit should move us. There are a bewildering number of holders offered, but let's start with a caveat: do not underestimate the force of a big fish's strike. It can easily snap plastic holders and/or pull out screws in which case you lose the rig over the side. Always use at least aluminum holders and bolt them in place.

One of the main functions of holders in a small boat is to extend the rods in a Y fashion to get more distance between the lines and thus lessen the chances of entangling on turns. (They will anyway.) The easiest way to achieve this is to bolt the holders on an angle to the transom. On some boats the back of the console seat can be used. If the holders will be in the way on a seat or transom or in a boat that has a transom seat in it, there are holders that are removable. I once had a boat I wanted to car-top. Yet to keep the reels high enough so they could be turned I wanted the ends of the holder to be above the gunwale. Holders on brackets solved the problem. A very popular holder mounts on a spade-shaped flathead. This slips into a very flat permanent bracket. You can buy extra permanent brackets and mount them so you have a variety of rod-positioning options. Although the holders are large and rather ungainly, it doesn't make any difference because they are stored when not actually working. Other holders are made to mount on rails. Many boats with low gunwales have rails around the cockpit. Drill the rail or use a V-bolt mount; a permanent mount goes on the rail. The holders are on or off as you desire.

The commonest holders are those that mount flush in the side decks in the cockpit. The actual butt tube is belowdecks out of sight. One problem with them is water. If they are not holed, the water will get in them and squish up at you when you stick a rod butt in. If you bore a hole in the bottom of the tube, rain and spray drain down in the same spot, pick up color from the metal, and leave an ugly dark line. In a wood boat the same factors can cause dry rot. The good thing about these holders is that they utilize otherwise unusable space and can't get in the way. Also you can stick in six or eight of them, which the coho boys do all the time. Their after cockpits look like a forest of spiny trees.

If you do much casting you may want a holder forward by the helmsman's seat. Some bass-boat guys mount a holder like this. They call it a rod tender, and it comes in handy when changing lures, unhooking fish, reaching for a beer. It's handy, too, because in some kinds of fishing you have only an instant to grab a rod and cast.

Outriggers

Let's get something straight at the start. The only purpose of an outrigger is to keep the baits spread wide apart so the lines won't foul on turns. You'll read that they were invented to impart a skipping motion to the bait and thus more closely imitate flying fish. 'Tain't so. If this was the case, the flatlines (lines that troll directly from the rod tips) wouldn't raise as many fish as the rigger lines, and they do. The late Tommy Gifford invented the outriggers in the late 1920s (along with kite fishing and the flying bridge) because he fished from a 26-foot Jersey skiff and needed distance between lines on so small a boat. The idea was quickly adopted by other charterboat skippers along the Long Island and Jersey coast because they liked to fish six people for bluefish. With this many lines dragging behind, you need *sloooow* turns and as much space between the baits as possible.

The outrigger function starts really with rod holders that extend the rods outboard as far as possible. The rods function as the rigger. At the other extreme are 25-foot Lee and Pompanette double spreader poles that with the deck and cabinside mounts will run you $1,500 before anyone starts drilling holes. For small boats most use removable holders with two- or three-position bases and 15-foot poles. You put the riggers

Riggers here come in over the Bimini top. A bit awkward to change positions, but you do it only twice a day. Rigger lines run to cockpit. Note good compass and fathometer placement and shielded lights. (Courtesy Slickcraft Boat Co.)

straight up for running and lay them at a shoulder angle or all the way flat while fishing. These cost around $150 and are good because you can quickly remove poles for trailering. I have seen these with side mounts that could be bolted to the sides of the console, but they are hard to find. Another trick is to mount them on the top of handhold rails around a console windshield or on Bimini towers.

The bad thing about outriggers, especially in a small boat, is that working four rods is a pain. It's almost impossible if you're alone. When you figure the beam of most mid-sized boats from 18 to 24 feet is 8 feet and you subtract 6 inches of deck on either side from that, the cockpit is only 7 feet wide. This is barely adequate for two men to move around in, much less handle the rods, pull down the rigger lines, and so forth. And if there is a lot of grass or action, four rods will keep you hopping.

When boats get small enough to sport only 5 or 6 feet of cockpit room, the problem of roominess becomes more acute. A pal of mine got a 17-foot Mako and wanted to mount riggers on it. I got both of us in the boat with a couple of rods and it was instantly apparent the four rods were just too many. I suppose you could compromise and mount one rigger and fish three rods, but I've never seen it done. The riggers are sold in pairs anyway.

The good things about outriggers are manifest. In the first place, they look salty as hell. Dress up any craft. They are the finest place in the world to fly flags from. Although it's strictly against nautical protocol, on ceremonial occasions I fly the ensign on the starboard side and my yacht-club burgee from the other. Traditionalists wince. I stand proud. Needless to say, no sport fisherman worth tinkerbelle would fly a flag from the stern, any more than he'd have raised cleats or a raised stern light there.

Outriggers offer an automatic (usually) dropback in billfishing. When a billfish strikes a bait with his bill, the bait is supposed to sink so the fish thinks he killed it. Then he swallows it. All this requires you to throw the reel in free spool and count to ten slowly while the billfish swallows the bait. In Baja they stop the boat, but in most cases the boat keeps moving. Therefore to sink the bait you must react instantly on a flatline reel and throw it in free spool. The fall from the rigger, *if* the billfish knocks the line out of the pin, will allow the bait to sink long enough for you to get to the rod and throw the click off and drop back some more. The reel should be in free spool with the click set to keep the spool from turning. Learning the timing of this backdrop is all-important. In Florida some boats use an automatic dropback device. This is like the drum of a large spinning reel. The line is wound on to allow what the skipper hopes is the right amount of dropback. A clip device keeps the line on the reel until the whack of a bill releases it.

There's no particular trick to mounting outriggers, aside from seeing that you have them on the right side. Both riggers and lines offer a fair amount of wind resistance. I use 80-pound-test Dacron line for the lines. Heavy monofilament line is also good.

One last word about outriggers. Don't forget they are there and run under a bridge, as my son did. "I knew you wouldn't be mad, Dad," he said. "Because I could see you doing exactly the same thing." I had to admit it was possible. This incidentally creates what are called *stub riggers*, that is, short poles that some small-boat skippers prefer anyway.

The large splash well in Claude Rogers' boat frequently finds itself full of channel bass.

Fish and Bait Storage

Storing frozen baits and fish you eventually want to eat used to pose problems aboard a small boat. These problems have largely been solved with the new plastic coolers. They are relatively inexpensive, come in a variety of sizes and colors, are easy to keep clean, and, best of all, really do the job. They provide excellent insulation. Baits go into one and are iced down along with the beer and Cokes. Valuable frozen baits will keep a long time in a cooler if you slip them in a smaller cooler, like a hand cooler, then put them on ice. Another trick is to buy a piece of dry ice on the way to the dock and keep that near them.

Edible-fish storage techniques vary. A lot of boats have built-in wells in the cockpit floor nowadays. These are okay for storing fish, of course, but they are mean to clean if you start leaving dead fish in them. A cooler is easier to clean, because you can take it on the dock to scrub out and not get the gore all over the cockpit. Speaking of gore, if you allow edible fish to lie in blood and slime their flavor will be ruined. You can rig a little platform in the cooler to keep them off the bottom. Another trick is to run a hose from the drain plug of the cooler out a scubbard. Sluice the fish down from time to time with fresh water, which flushes the gore away and keeps the fish fresh. Lacking an overboard drain, run the hose into the bilge with a couple of bucketfuls of water and some detergent to mix it with. When you clean up after the fishing, out goes the gore in much-diluted form.

Another good thing about a cooler is that you can outsmart "dirty" fish that spew gore all over (bluefish are notorious for this). You get the fish alongside, open the cooler, pop him in it, and quickly shut the lid. He can thump all he wants. The gore remains in the cooler.

Here's a fish flopper stopper I learned from New Orleans anglers. Keep a wet piece of burlap that is old enough to have lost any smell spread out on the floor of the cockpit aft. It lies flat, and you can walk on it. On hot days it cools your tootsies. When a fish comes aboard, swing it immediately onto the burlap and instantly wrap the fish in the wet cloth. Know what happens? The fish in that warm, wet embrace just lies there perfectly still and dies. No flips and flops. No muss, no fuss.

A splash well in front of the outboard makes a good adjunct to the cooler and/or gore problem. A spacious splash well can take a good large fish, and, of course, all wells drain overboard. Fish can be kept in them covered by wet burlap. A splash well is the best place in the world for stinky half-rotten bait. Much better than storing it in an empty live well and forgetting it until notified by the aroma two weeks later.

Another edible-fish storage trick I used for years was a regular plastic garbage can. I'd stick bluefish and striped bass in it nose-down to defeat the don't-store-in-the-gore problem. The can is cheap, washes out easily, and can be pressed into actual garbage service in its declining years.

Live Wells

As noted, many boats have live wells built into the cockpit floor. I have to fill mine by hand, and it drains into the bilge. Others incorporate a complicated plumbing system that can, if something like a hose clamp lets go, sink the boat. This happened to me off Walker Key and all hands had an exciting fifteen minutes or so saving a brand-new $25,000 rig from taking a dive.

Wells aren't as bothersome to clean if you are using them according to their designed purpose and not to store fish. They will be filled with water then, of course, and live bait isn't as messy as dead fish. And in elaborate rigs, fresh water is circulating in them at all times. This keeps cleaning problems to a minimum.

A sturdy cooler also serves admirably as a live well, especially with a block of ice in it to help keep water temperatures down. (When water heats up, it loses its oxygen.) Some people use the little battery aerators on coolers. The same thing is true with plastic garbage cans that make a fair live-bait storage spot. The self-tending outboard live wells used in the Keys that are boxes mounted on the transom are nifty. They use them mostly with shrimp, which are fairly easy to catch with your hand. With live fish, you'd probably have to get yourself a little net or lose some to squirming free.

Go-Deep Rigs

Going deep after fish with wire or lead lines requires no customizing. Planners, too, present no problems. But the best way of deep fishing, raised to a high art by the coho crew, utilizes downriggers. These do need some planning and particulars. Downriggers are no more than cannonball weights dropped to predetermined depths on aircraft-cable wires. The wires are wound on reels that are bolted to the deck along the transom and sides of the boat. An extender arm from a few inches to 4 feet in length acts as a mini-outrigger. The actual fishing line clips to the cannonball, similarly to the way it goes on an outrigger line. When a fish hits, the lines pull free. A counter is on the drum, so you can return lines to exact depths. There's no particular trick to mounting the downriggers, and all I know of have permanent mounts that go on the deck. Reels and arms are removable. They are efficient things, but ugly. Costs depend on degree of sophistication. Simpler ones have a handle on the reel and wind manually. However, you soon "gits weary and sick o' tryin'" reeling in the 10-pound cannonball all day long and will want an electric motor to do it for you, at a cost of $50 or more. Counters that spell out how deep the cannonball is also vary in sophistication.

The way the coho boys do it for salmon and (mostly) lake trout is to cruise until fish are spotted on the depthsounder. Then lures go down and are set to "cover" the depth at which the fish are lying. If the schools are at 35 feet, you'll set a lure at 30 feet, several at 35, a couple at 40. You see now why coho addicts fish six rods as standard and more as needed. Don't we have fun when the fish hit in bunches and start running every which way.

Back Trolling

Back trolling is a technique worked out by walleye trollers in Michigan. These guys go at dead-slow speeds and need to pinpoint lures through precise areas. Backtrolling is based on the fact that it's easier to control a boat by pulling it than pushing it. This is why bass-boat electrics are mounted on the bow. Another factor is that outboard thrust bearings in reverse are the same as forward and no damage is done to the machines. You don't want to hit anything, though, as the tilt-up protection is obviously gone. There's no particular trick to backtrolling, and you can turn the boat around if need be and all the fishermen need do is switch directions. Since transoms will kick up water in a chop, habitués of this art rig splash panels on both sides of the motor. These can be made of light plywood, truck panels, aluminum, canvas, or even burlap sheets on aluminum or wood frames. Your ingenuity will design them for your boat.

Tackle and Lure Storage

If you are a normal fisherman, your supply of fishing accoutrements will be immense. Extra lines, and lead lines and wire, and spare parts for reels, and spare guides, and hooks in infinite variety — different sizes and styles, both snelled and unsnelled, etc. — and an assortment of weights and sinkers — eggs, ovals, pyramids in various ounce sizes — and swivels and snaps in a dozen sizes and kinds, including some sprayed flat black for toothy fish that will strike shiny brass swivels and cut your lines, and leader wire in several tests, and coils of heavy monofilament for leaders, and fishermen pliers (a safety need if somebody gets hooked besides a fish), and fly-tying material — feathers, bucktails, whatever — and nylon hair with suitable paints for making your own lures or modifying others, and plastic molds and pots and pourers to mold your own plastic worms and wiggle lures. The list is growing larger, and we haven't even got to the most important part. The number of lures you'll collect is limited only by your pocketbook and/or ingenuity. Look at the mass of gear you've assembled already.

The sheer mass is an enormity. Then if you fish both fresh and salt water as I do, you will probably sooner or later split the gear into two parts and keep them separate, simply because saltwater usage is so tough on stuff. Use freshwater lures in salt and they

Ingenious use of otherwise wasted space is made possible through stowage seats. Cabinet holds lures and rigs in boxes. Port seat box contains a Porta-Pottie. (Courtesy Jack Olson)

are darn near one-time-only shots. At today's lure prices, rust will eat you up. So you go to gear — rods, reels, lures — specifically intended for freshwater or saltwater work.

Then if you fish for marlin, fish the flats, the surf, cast to jetties, pop after snook and trout, your tackle has to be somewhat organized and separated for each category. Fresh water has the same problems. Fly gear doesn't use the same lures, lines, et al. as spinning. Even similar tackle differs. For example, trout fly-rod gear differs from bass fly-rod gear.

Somehow you've got to make some sense out of all this. There has to be some rudimentary organization so you can get the stuff from the pile that you need today, and, more important, get it back in the same place so you can find it tomorrow.

If you have a big enough boat you can build in lockers. These may go in along the sides under the deck. You can make one in the space under a seat. I built shelves along the sides of the cuddy. Drawers are good for storage. The see-through plastic boxes further organize gear within the storage areas. When you are building storage areas, keep Plexiglas in mind. The stuff can be sawed and drilled like wood, and its see-through qualities show you the contents of bins, drawers, etc. at a glance.

In small boats or console boats, gear must go in compartments — big boxes. Generally there is storage under a seat forward of the console, under the helmsman's seat, and in one or more stowage compartments built in forward or aft. These latter often leave a lot to be desired as stowage spots because they sweat. Gear is always damp, and that's no way to store equipment in salt water or fresh.

The new tackle boxes help with the stowage dilemma. Used to be if you got a box big enough to store all the gear you needed, you could never find what you were looking for without a struggle. Now the sides of the boxes open up into the famous drawer-stowage methods. You in effect have a removable drawer locker. The box comes and goes with the skipper and when not working sits in the dehumidified air of the air conditioner, which keeps the rust problem to a minimum.

If your boat is too small even for seat or console compartments, you can always make use of the ubiquitous coolers. Get some of the flat plastic boxes and store them in the cooler along with spare lines, beer in a bucket, and so forth.

Big-Fish Techniques

This section is saltwater oriented. You don't catch mankillers in fresh water, but there is every likelihood on the sea that you'll take leave of your senses and bait, catch, and kill a 450-pound, man-eating shark before it kills you. My friend Al Restori did just that, landing a 450-pound Mako shark out of a 19-foot Mako boat. When you have a huge and exceedingly angry animal like that alongside, the danger from it is very real. Giant tuna and big marlin are not as menacing as a shark, but their very size is perilous. Get a line around your finger or hand and over the side goes you (or your finger) — make no mistake about it. Bring a 200-pound tuna into a small boat in too green — that is, still full of fight — condition, and he will scramble the interior even while you're doing a war dance trying to get into position to belt him. Make it a 200-pound marlin shaking an exceedingly lethal sword from side to side and you'll do well to keep in mind the maneuver utilized by Florida charterboat skippers when an unknowing soul brings a moray eel into the boat. The knowledgable skippers go over the side!

Nets and Gaffs

A net is the safest way to land a fish. You immerse the net into the water and lead the fish to it with the fish's nose facing it. Then you scoop up the fish. Never approach from the tail. The inclination of a frightened, albeit weakened, fish is to spurt ahead, and in the facing position the fish tends to dive into the net. Never, never try to scoop the fish up in one big lunge. You'll hit the fish and knock it off the hook.

The major trouble with nets is that they are for relatively small fish only. The biggest nets I know of are made for striped bass. They may have an opening several feet in diameter and handle fish up to 4 and 5 feet. When you get 40 or 50 pounds at the end of a long handle you don't exactly flip it out of the water. It's enough to slip the fish into the pocket and pull the net to the boat's side, where a couple of hands can lift the fish into the cockpit.

One problem with nets is that they are impossible to stow, and more in the way the bigger they are. If you are using lures with multiple hooks, such as a jointed Pikie minnow with three trebles, you'll spend some good fishing time unhooking the fish, then untangling the hooks from the net.

A gaff is quick and neat and has the advantage of hurting, even killing, a fish before it gets into the boat. The proper technique is to slip the gaff in the water and lay the fish over it, then impale it with a sharp yank. This way, if you miss you miss. Never try to strike down on a fish as if you were digging with a pickax. It's astonishing how often you'll miss the fish this way and knock the lure out of its mouth.

You have to match the size of the gaff to the size of the fish. The arc of the hook should be about half the side dimensions of the fish you are gaffing. This way when you set the gaff under the fish—actually, what you do is lead the fish over the gaff—you are striking into the middle of its side, and if you miss, as you will, it will still catch in either the back or belly. It's easy to have several different sizes of gaffs because the hooks can be bought separately and wrapped on a suitable shaft.

You can gaff as big a fish as you can lift with a rigid gaff, but when you get much over 100 pounds, most go to a flying gaff. The simplest kind of flying gaff is a rigid gaff with a hole through its head through which a light rope is threaded. If the gaffed fish overpowers you and swims away—not an uncommon occurrence—you can let the line go, snubbing it around a cleat (not too hard or you'll pull the hook), then leading the fish back to where you can regain the shaft.

The most sophisticated flying gaffs have a detachable hook so the shaft falls away. There are several reasons for this. First, if the fish leaps, you sure don't want the shaft acting as a club flying around over your head. Second, the shaft is clumsy in the water, and its drag makes handling the package more difficult than need be. Third, as the fish lurches, a shaft in the water acts as a level trying to pull the hook.

I rigged up a 14-foot Starcraft as a boat to use on stories. There's a cooler to keep beer and/or fish. Garbage can next to it is dry stowage. A rope keeps the top from straying. Behind this are twin 6-gallon tanks. Main outboard is 25 with an auxiliary 7½. Bow light and sternlight are battery-powered and removable.

Here's how you handle a big fish. The angler fights him until the double line comes aboard. This is immediately grabbed and the fish handlined within gaffable range. At this point the angler gets out of the chair and/or out of the way and puts the reel on light drag. Then someone sticks the fish with the gaff. This often causes a last desperate run, and the light drag allows the fish to take line without tearing the hook out of its mouth.

The fish is brought alongside by hauling on the rope to the flying gaff. Here it is belted with a billy or pacifier, which is nothing more than a small baseball bat with a thong around it to keep it from slipping out of your hand. The fish is smacked as hard as possible right over the eyes. Often at this point a noose is slipped over its tail for added insurance against escape.

After the fish is dead, there are several options, depending on the size of the fish and whether or not it is a shark. If you can bring a nondangerous fish aboard, do so. Larger boats have gin poles to help lift big fish. A gin pole is simply a pole high enough to which you can hitch a block and tackle. On fancy sportfishermen, a transom door opens in the transom, the deck is wetted down, and the monsters slide into the cockpit.

On small boats the sides are low enough that several people can manhandle aboard fish up to 300 pounds or so. If you get a fish larger than this, there is no recourse but to lash it alongside. Truss the fish up with its head as high as possible facing the bow. Lash the tail securely and home you come. On Hawaii's Kona coast they regularly catch marlin over 1,000 pounds out of 16- and 17-footers.

With big sharks there are a few extra exciting steps. In the first place, when you hit a shark with a gaff it may well attack the boat, actually bite at the side. You must be

Permanent anchor mount is in bow. Shock cord holds the shank securely.

prepared for this. Sharks are generally fought longer, so they are more exhausted alongside. Nobody in his right mind uses fast-catch techniques on sharks.

After the shark is gaffed, the best way to dispatch the same is to shoot it. The best weapon is a bang stick—a stick on a pole that fires a 12-gauge load of No. 4 shot when it is plunged against the fish's side. This kills any shark instantly. Next best is to shoot it with anything from a .22 on up. Despite what you read, all the sharks I've seen shot this way have cooled down rapidly. If you're fishing for records, shooting would disqualify the fish and you have no choice but to hammer on its head. Trouble is, while most other fish shudder and die under the blows, sharks tend to lie there wondering how to bite the thing. They take a lot of clubbing.

Now the fun begins, because you can never quite tell when a shark is dead. It's best to slip a noose over its tail and tow it for ten minutes or so to reverse the water through its gills and drown it. After this you can decide if you dare to bring it aboard, keeping in mind that if it does revive it will thrash wildly, clashing its jaws at anything they can come in contact with.

To lash a shark alongside, hook it in the mouth with the gaff and use this line to lash it forward. A tail noose holds it tightly from astern. Then even if it revives, the fish is held securely.

Sighting Aids

Spotting fish, or fish sign, is important in all fishing. Anglers are led to many saltwater species by birds working, surface agitation, color change, or spray as fish slash at bait at the surface. The ultimate in spotting comes in flats fishing for tarpon and bonefish, where in most cases you cast only to fish you see.

But keeping an eye on what's going on around you figures in freshwater fishing. Seeing a band of bait jumping, the swirl of a bass taking something on top, or the long, lean, underwater shadow of a musky—all can fill the fish box faster.

The first sighting aid is to stand up. Console boats build this in automatically. Many conventional windshield boats sport impromptu flying bridges—skipper sits on top of the back of his seat instead of down in it. In smaller boats an extension handle on the outboard allows you to stand and run the boat. The trouble with standing up is it can be dangerous. I always rigged a handhold rope on my little boats. I made it a rule never to conn the vessel without a hand around the rope. A lot of times guys will stand up on a seat or even the top of the console for a better look. Always stop the boat when you do this if you're alone.

As boats get bigger—over 24 feet and with ample beam, 10 feet or more—flying bridges offer an unexcelled sighting position. It's amazing how such a relatively modest elevation increases visibility. In the old days guys rigged an ersatz flying bridge by cutting a hatch in the cabin rooftop right over the wheel. The skipper then sat on the cabintop and steered with his feet. It serves as an effective height increaser that is far cheaper than the $4,000 or $5,000 that a bridge costs today.

Tuna or Bimini towers are popular today. They were developed at Bimini to spot schools of giant tuna in the clear waters, hence the name. Most are custom rigged to the boat, welded out of aluminum pipe. Since stresses on them are severe, they should be bolted to the boat with special backing plates of plywood to spread the loads. If bolted to side decks they somewhat defeat the purpose of a console, which is to provide walk-around room for casting. Some can be mounted on the sides of the console or even the sides of the boats. Again, throughbolts should be used throughout.

The towers look salty as all get out, to be sure, but I can't see many applications where they earn the $5,000 or so to stand one aloft. I put them in the class with gin poles and radar domes. For every dozen on board for status's sake, one gets actually used. In rough weather, stay out of towers—period.

A recent innovation for the flats is what might be called a poling-sighting platform. It is a small raised deck over the outboard on which the poler stands. How high it is depends on how long a pole the poler can handle. The platform adds windage and is a little weird-looking, but it is effective.

Here's a salty-looking tower that even has rod racks so the man upstairs gets to fish too. Note gin pole to port.

Bow platforms are flat decks built up in the very bow of the boat. They lift the fisherman slightly for better sighting and provide a secure area for casting. These came about mostly in the flyrod boom for big tarpon. To cast the long sticks you need a good place to set both feet firmly, as well as an uncluttered deck on which to lay surplus line without danger of it tangling.

Fishing Aids

There are a number of small but necessary items you'll need on board a fishing boat. One of the nicest is a plier and knife rack somewhere out in the open. Both these tools are in constant need, sometimes at a second's notice, and it shows a seasoned skipper to display them in proper place.

Soaps and cleaners along with mop, scrub brush, and buckets are another fishing must. I fussed with cheap supermarket plastic buckets that split or shed their handles. Then I found a farm-supply store and bought a couple of stainless steel milking buckets, and I am now the envy of all. Cleaning gear stows well in those damp lockers mentioned earlier because they are mostly stored in plastic containers. I've fooled with fiberglass cleaners, but find that the abrasive bleaches such as Comet and Bon Ami take stains out better.

If you trail your boat, a nifty way to clean it is to haul it to one of the car washes and scrub down with hot soapy water, then a hot rinse. Easy, efficient, and well worth the couple of bucks.

Cutting baits requires a board to keep from scarring up the afterdeck. Best way for this is to glue a board to the top of your cooler. Loose boards have a way of escaping overboard and — at least with me — I can never remember I need another board until I'm in the middle of the bay and find I don't have it.

CRC and WD-40 were unknown yesterday, yet are totally indispensable aboard a boat today. I spray everything about once every two weeks. By everything I mean the outboard (with cowl removed), all the wiring, cleats, stainless-steel rails, running lights, control handles, rods and reels, ignition switch, aluminum rails under helmsman's seat. I don't take the electronics apart and spray the works but probably should. Gunning from small boats in salt water is especially hard on shotguns, because they are in spray all the time and often get a bucketful over them. At the end of the day I take mine apart and put the barrel(s) right under the hottest water and wash it. I swab down the receivers with a sponge. Then I dry everything and spray with WD-40 or CRC. Haven't had a drop of oil on my guns in years. If there is a difference between the two (or their imitators for that matter), I can't see it.

Curtains

In case you've noticed, new materials have made what used to be called cockpit canvas into something that can really aid the fisherman. Soft tops and side and cockpit curtains today are vinyl, stitching is Dacron, zippers are (or should be) oversize brass

More modern curtains incorporate lots of clear plastic. In a boat this size — about 22 feet — they provide a warm dry area in all but torrential spray or rain.

or plastic, and see-through spots are provided by clear vinyl. Unlike the curtains of only a few years ago, the new ones are rugged and long-lasting.

There are a couple of types of curtains that work well on a console boat. The Bimini top that folds is the most common. They fasten to the sides of the boat and can be folded flat for stowage. The trouble with them is the rods or support straps reduce the openness of the boat. If you have to fight a big fish that leads you 360 degrees around the boat, you'll be forced to pass the rod around them.

A compromise is a flat top that sits over the console. This attaches to the sides of the console. It provides some sun relief, a spot of shade that at times can be gratefully received.

Full shell-like curtains over the forward part of the vessel can take much of the exposure factor out of console boats. I was in Cozumel in a 24-foot Mako that had a full forward curtain rigged, and it made a nifty cabin forward. You could have stayed dry in it through a downpour. Curtains today can be fitted on rod runners so they fold forward. No fishing boat wants the kind that folds on the aft transom.

The best enclosure comes with conventional windshield boats. The soft so-called "Navy" top keeps out the spray. Then if you rig clear side curtains you'll find the area stays really warm. And of course you can enclose the whole cockpit and turn the afterdeck into a watertight weatherproof cabin.

12

Customizing Bass Boats and Striper Boats

Bass boats are the exception to the customizing rule that to get it the way you want it, you must do it yourself. These are such specialized machines that the builder-dealers are capable of doing it all for you. Lockers, rod holders, live wells, battery box, gas tank locker, instruments, running lights, horn, fuse panel, wheel, custom seats—all are standard on most boats. However, there are some special considerations to bass boating that are worth discussing.

Morning mist frames a bass boat at work. Explosive growth of such a specialized vessel is unprecedented in all boating's history.

Here's the ultimate in tournament fishermen. Sterndrive provides super power for top performance. But does the higher horsepower and lighter weight of the big outboards make this breed obsolete?

Tournament Boat vs. Fishing Machine

There isn't any question that bass boats have arrived as status symbols. The sparkle
finishes prove that if the fancy prices don't. Now, if you've made it big and want the
world to know, that's okay with me. Where the confusion comes — I think — is differ-
entiating between a boat that is designed to be competitive in tournaments and a fishing
machine aimed solely at having fun.

To win any major tournament a bass boat has got to be fast and powerful. This
means big — at least 16 or 17 feet, with the highest horsepower. And, of course, all fancy
live-well arrangements with aerators and water circulation are included in the package. The reason you need a boat like this is that most tournaments are held on lakes

big enough to take the fishing pressure without too much criticism being directed at the participants or sponsor. In a big impoundment it is quite conceivable you may want to fish one spot now and another area that appeals to you later and the two might be miles apart. You need a boat that can gobble up those miles and not waste fishing time.

Naturally, these big tournament boats come with a price to match their performance. It's perfectly possible to spend $10,000 for a boat, motor, and trailer today. That's a lot of money for a vessel designed to do just one thing.

But do you actually plan to fish tournaments? Many object to the whole idea of making fishing into a competitive sport. If you fish brushy bayous, reedy lakes, or small streams, there is an advantage to a smaller boat. The price is half tournament costs or less. Smaller and lighter makes launching and loading easier. The boat draws less water. Gas bills go down.

One of the things I like about the smaller rigs is that stick steering is safe with them. A stick gives you infinitely more maneuverability, and it allows you to conn the vessel from the forward pedestal seat. Over about 20 mph or so, the sticks simply aren't safe. It's too easy to be thrown in a too-hard turn, or you can fall against the stick and flip the boat. The safety of a console that you can sit behind is needed at higher speeds.

Of course, if you want others on your block to look up to you, that's your business. However, it must be stated that the glamour of a beat-up 1957 pickup hauling a week-old $8,000 bass boat is not to be denied.

Striper Boats

The success of stocking freshwater striped bass has created an offshoot of the bass boat called striper boats. Regular bass boats can and are used to go after these exciting

This is the other extreme, just a fancied-up johnboat, but able to compete seriously in a tournament and with a realistic price tag.

This striper boat, designed to catch freshwater striped bass now being stocked all over the country, reflects the requirements of the sport: removable outriggers for trolling, pads aft for downrigger or deep trolling, number of rigged rods at ready for various kinds of fishing, and storage in helmsman seat and passenger seat forward of the console. Since stripers are usually found in big water, the boat is somewhat huskier than most bass boats.

fish, but the fishing demands are causing many fishermen to customize new rigs. In the first place, stripers can be large; 40-pounders are not unknown, so big ice wells and bait wells are needed. The supersize coolers will do — if there's a place for them.

You catch freshwater stripers in three different ways. First, they form schools on the surface and can be spotted and cast to, which suggests a standup console and open boat for casting. Second, they are trolled for deep. Again deck pads on the stern are needed to handle downriggers. The pads should be removable for when the boat is used for bass fishing. Third, many are caught deep, on jigs at night. Good lights that don't shine on the water — a fatal error — are in order. Bass boat similarities are the need for speed, range, live wells for bait and smaller fish (striper tournaments are starting), lockable rod storage, electrics, and electronics. In the future, bass and striper boats may have interiors whose components can be changed — removable pedestals, for example.

Kevlar vs. Fiberglass

Another bass-boat choice you'll have to investigate is whether you want to pay the premium for Kevlar. Kevlar is a Du Pont–developed fiber that by weight is stronger than steel. By using less of the stronger fiber (in combination with fiberglass), a weight reduction is possible. Hydra-Sport, a Nashville-based builder, pioneered Kevlar use. The company found that it could build a 15-foot bass boat that weighed 550 pounds versus the same boat in fiberglass at 650 pounds. The same 20 to 25 percent weight saving with no loss of strength holds for larger boats. The increase in cost, however, is considerable — around $400 for 15-footers to over $500 for larger bassers. However, the company to date has built some 2,000 boats and its sales are over 90 percent Kevlar. The stuff is worth looking at.

New Designs

Bass boats long ago outgrew their generally flat bottom and began to take on all manner of new shapes. The latest fad is the so-called "pad" boats. These lift the whole vessel out of the water at high speeds. By running on a smaller section of the bottom — the so-called pad — friction is reduced and higher speeds are attainable. The day of the 60-mph bass boat has been with us for many years, and the pad is increasing the fleet.

The trouble with many of these boats is that they get quite "squirrelly" on the pad. That is, they wiggle and feel as if they are going to tip over. In fact, plenty of them do tip over or go out of control. When that happens at 60 mph or even 40 mph, injuries and damages are certain. It's a good rule never to buy *any* boat you haven't personally checked out. Take a demonstration ride or ask around and get the scoop from guys who own one. It's particularly true today in the bass-boat field because there has been so much change and innovation, sometimes without adequate testing time on the part of the manufacturer.

By way of emphasizing my point, I was at a meeting of the nation's top boating writers. A friend of mine got out of a newly designed bass boat and asked that I take a ride in it and tell him what I thought. The boat was beautiful up to about 40 mph. Beyond that the thing frankly scared the hell out of me. It felt as though the torque (twisting force of the prop) alone was trying to capsize the boat. If you hit a wave or wake and allowed the boat to become airborne, the chance of it flipping was more than I would dare risk. I so reported to my pal, and he agreed. The boat had frightened him too.

Always take a ride first.

Here are some of the things to keep in mind with the small amount of customizing you may want to do.

Fire Extinguisher

Fire extinguishers get used on bass boats more often than on other boats because of all the batteries and electric wiring. Also, on many bass boats, outboard tanks are put in lockers where fumes can collect.

Electric Outboard

One of the first customizing considerations is mounting the electric outboard. This should present no problem in the physical mounting. All bass boats have a wide, flat forward deck designed to take the motor mount. All you have to do is drill bolts for the deck mount of your particular machine and fasten the bolts down. The trend in boats today is to provide wiring for the motor. The wiring is no great problem once you have a good diagram. The main complaints come with the 24-volt motors, since there are no 24-volt chargers and you have to split the load so you can charge with 12-volt chargers. Add to this the potential of 24-volt burnout. If at any time you shoot 24 volts into your outboard it will burn out the powerpack instantly. Some $250 later you'll be running again. The trend today is toward the heavy thrust 12-volt electrics. Mercury started with their redesign several years ago. Now all the electric companies offer them. They get the job done without the hassles and batteries of the 24's.

Batteries

The word is getting around now, but to make sure let's emphasize that there are two kinds of batteries — cranking and deep-cycle. Turning your main outboard over to start it requires cranking power. The Sears Diehard is a good crank battery. But repeatedly charging and discharging this kind of battery will greatly shorten its life. To run your electric outboard requires a deep-cycle battery that has much thicker grids and can be repeatedly charged without damage. The Gould battery people are leading the industry in publicizing the differences in the two kinds, and they offer good batteries in both categories.

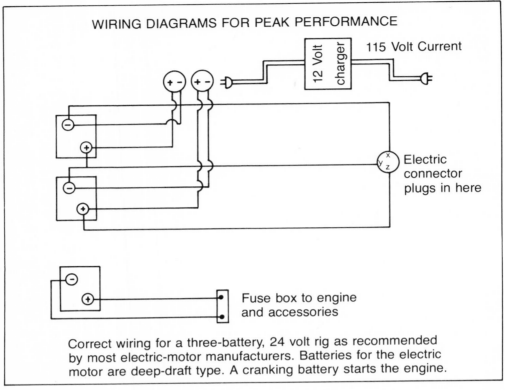

WIRING DIAGRAMS FOR PEAK PERFORMANCE

Correct wiring for a three-battery, 24 volt rig as recommended by most electric-motor manufacturers. Batteries for the electric motor are deep-draft type. A cranking battery starts the engine.

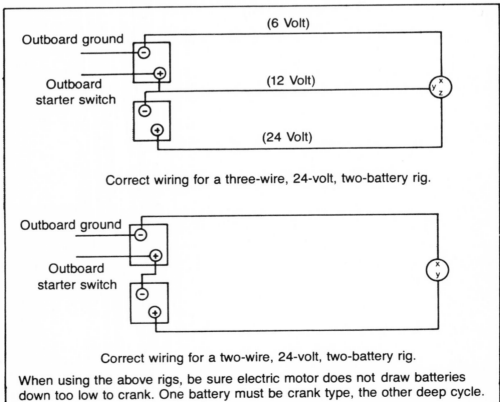

Correct wiring for a three-wire, 24-volt, two-battery rig.

Correct wiring for a two-wire, 24-volt, two-battery rig.

When using the above rigs, be sure electric motor does not draw batteries down too low to crank. One battery must be crank type, the other deep cycle.

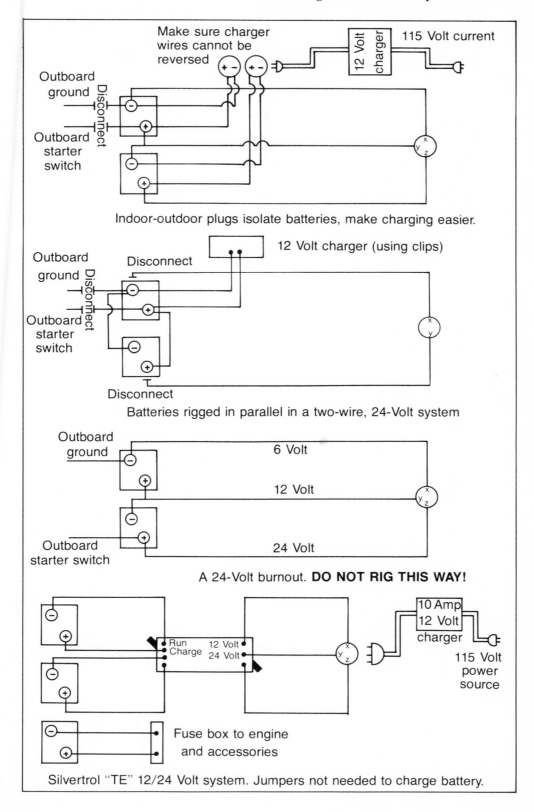

Make sure charger wires cannot be reversed

12 Volt charger

115 Volt current

Outboard ground

Disconnect

Outboard starter switch

Indoor-outdoor plugs isolate batteries, make charging easier.

12 Volt charger (using clips)

Outboard ground

Disconnect

Outboard starter switch

Disconnect

Batteries rigged in parallel in a two-wire, 24-Volt system

Outboard ground

6 Volt

12 Volt

24 Volt

Outboard starter switch

A 24-Volt burnout. **DO NOT RIG THIS WAY!**

Run Charge

12 Volt
24 Volt

10 Amp 12 Volt charger

115 Volt power source

Fuse box to engine and accessories

Silvertrol "TE" 12/24 Volt system. Jumpers not needed to charge battery.

Depthsounder

The next bass-boat essential will be a depthsounder. You may want two flasher stations — one at the wheel and one that can be read from the forward fishing chair. Both can work from the same transducer. However, with the two flashers I'd rig one transducer all the way aft for high-speed reading and one taped to the bottom of the electric trolling motor. This way you'll have two complete systems backing each other. Tricks on installing transducers are covered in the chapter on electronics.

CB Radio

CBs have finally arrived in bass-boat country. There is nothing particular to bass boating about them. See how to rig them in the chapter on electronics.

Automatic Bilge Pump

An automatic bilge pump is a definite safety factor. Any expensive boat should be equipped with one. No particular problems to them — except they break down all the time. Again, bass-boat builders have been trying so hard to solve the wiring problems caused by the electric motor that your boat will probably come with a good fuse panel. Run the pump wires from the panel.

Boat Reins

These are spring-loaded reels that stow dock lines belowdecks. They are strictly for bass boats and are handy to keep things neat. There are no tricks to installation beyond drilling the hole through the deck in a place where you can get at the underside of the deck as well as the top. Then the reels are bolted in place.

Anchors

For really precision fishing you should have anchors fore and aft. Then once you've found a honey hole you can fish right on top of it. Again, there are no problems involved beyond drilling and bolting mounts. You can use an electric winch, but unless you plan on doing a lot of anchoring it is hardly worth the money. Reeling by hand is faster, and you'll use less current and never break down. One thing you want to be sure of with all anchors is that they come equipped with a secure locking device that holds the anchors in place while running. If an anchor should release at high speed it could wreck your vessel and possibly yourself.

Kill Switch

Most newer bass boats have a switch that attaches to the driver's belt. If the switch is pulled, it stops the boat. This is a must device because of the high running speeds of which most bass boats are capable and the stump-ridden waters in which most operate. People get thrown from them all the time. Both OMC and Mercury offer easy-to-install kill-switch kits.

Spot and Interior Lights

A spotlight is a useful accessory because sooner or later you'll be in hot fishing action, unwilling to quit until darkness overtakes you. The best spotlights for bass boats are those that mount permanently but feature a removable slip socket. This way you aim it so it shows the water ahead by steering the boat. Yet when you need light for fishing, the spot can be removed and aimed by hand. There are a few super flashlights that serve as spotlights yet can be changed into floodlights for working in the cockpit.

As mentioned elsewhere, small dome lights low in the boat are a fishing aid. They can be rigged so that no light falls on the surface of the water — a fishing no-no — yet you can reach down and get light on a lure or fish. No problem either to find or install.

Windshields

Bass boaters tend to fish all winter in those areas of the country where waters don't freeze. Usually they protect their faces with motorcycle, snowmobiler, or welder's helmets. Investigate the potential of a windshield fabricated out of Plexiglas. Sometimes even a small one can give surprising protection when you hunch down behind it.

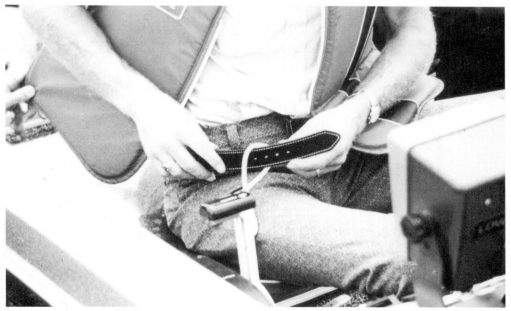

An essential item in a boat fast enough to throw the operator is a kill switch that shuts down the engine instantly and prevents boat from circling.

Trailer Customizing

For some reason bass boaters are usually willing to buy good trailers for their boats. These come well equipped. Since boats are loaded and launched by immersing the trailer, customizing is only to protect against the effects of water. The first thing is to protect hubs. Inner bearings are heated to high temperatures by spinning along the road. When these are immersed in the relatively cold water, the air in the hub compresses and sucks in water. This eventually causes the bearings to rust. Bearing Buddies fit on the outside of the hubs and prevent this. If they go under you want to ensure that trailer lights are waterproof. They should be plastic, with neoprene seals. Another good idea for a trailer is to install a plywood plank deck so you can walk down the trailer to get to the boat without falling overboard.

Newest interior designs are called combination boats. Seats open the boat and make them useful to take passengers along.

13
Electronics

Marine electronics long ago left the category of gadgetry. Reliable and inexpensive aids are widely available. What's more, they work! Some are fishing aids, some safety items, others just keep you in touch with your breaker, breaker buddies.

Fish Finders

There isn't any question you'll catch more fish with a so-called fish finder. Thousands have been using them for years. No pro would set sail without one. Anyone could make a case for depthsounders (the more correct name) on the basis that they show you the bottom contours of the waters you fish. Instead of fishing blind you can concentrate on the underwater points, ledges, steps, humps, and rises that are the favored position of all fish in fresh or salt water. But depthsounders in this day of electronic miracles can do much more than that. They give important clues as to the nature of the bottom, reveal individual fish as well as schools, and can even mark the progress of your lure down to them! Indispensable? I guess so!

Fish finders work by sending out a continuous 4,800-feet-per-second signal from a cigarette-sized unit called a transducer that is mounted in the water and connected by wire to the finder. The transducer signal fans out in a cone until it hits something. Then, like a radar pulse, it bounces back. The instrument measures the amount of time it takes to send and receive the signal and translates this into linear measurement — that is, the depth of the water. Fine instruments costing several thousand dollars can read to 500 fathoms or more and are utilized by offshore commercial fishing vessels — hence the name *fathometer*. More common versions selling for less than $100 can read to 200 feet before they lose sensitivity.

In addition to measuring the depth of water, fish finders tell you other things. The signal "bounces" off changes in density. Rocks are quite a bit denser than mud, sand is denser than mud but not as dense as rock, and so on. When the signal bounces off rock

One of the fisherman's most important tools is his depthsounder. But CB radio is a safety item that adds to the fun too.

it translates into a crisp line on the face of your finder. When it mushes into mud the recording line will be broad. If there are underwater plants or trees, where, as a common example, a forest has been flooded, they will appear as "ghosts," flickers, and flecks above the bottom. With a little experience, the difference in your signal will tell you quite a bit about what kind of bottom you are fishing over. At certain times this can be vital fishing information. And since in a proper installation the signal will read as well at 30 mph as 3 mph, you can scout at high speeds to find exactly the kind of bottom or structure you want.

All fish have an air bladder that is less dense than the water it displaces. When the electronic signal hits this, it responds with a weak reply signal that shows up in various ways on your machine. If there is one great big fish, the signal will be strong. If there is a school of many little fish, you can recognize it from the "ghost" effect.

Sounders are used to locate individual fish or schools of fish more in salt water than fresh. This is because salt water is comparatively so much vaster. Fishermen can and do cruise until they locate the fish and only then put over their lines. In fresh water, fish will show as well. At times this is a useful tool. When crappie fishing in spring, for example, you will probably do better to locate a school before you fish. The fish finder will aid this. More often the finder locates the habitat a certain species prefers. Where exactly does the weed line end? That's where you want to cast or troll for pike or pickerel. Is there a rocky hump underwater or a sharp rock dropoff? That's where the smallmouth will be found.

While finders are useful in all kinds of fishing, bass fishermen brought them to their peak of utilization. They are especially important in the great impoundments of the south and west. The foundations of homes razed before the waters backed up are prime bass sites, as are old road and railroad right-of-ways that are now submerged. Find points with dropoffs and the bass will move up and down them as light and water temperatures change. The beds of the rivers and feeder tributaries before they were dammed particularly are hotspots.

So useful a fishing tool is even the least expensive fish finder that it is safe to say almost any fisherman equipped with one will outfish the angler without. When you consider that the more expensive models ranging in the $500 to $1,000 area are so sensitive they will pick out not only individual fish but your lure heading down toward it, their importance to the whole fishing picture is clear.

There are a number of different types of sounders; one is of little value to fishermen.

DIGITAL. These read the distance to the bottom in numbers like a digital watch. They are extremely easy to read, especially for those who need glasses to read the smaller numbers on the other types. However, they do not give vital bottom information, nor will fish show on them.

FLASHERS. These have a round face, and a small neon light flashes to indicate the depth and type of bottom. A soft bottom will appear as a band of light a quarter-inch wide or more, rock as a narrow, fine-line band. Fish show up as ticks of light between the bottom and the boat. Schools of fish show up as a number of blips, sometimes a "shower" of little lights, and if the school is huge and thick, a second solid band may show. The disadvantages of the flashers are that you must be looking at them at all times to see the activity, and, despite sun shields, they can be hard to read in bright sunlight.

RECORDERS. These make a permanent record of depth, bottom info, and fish (if any) on a moving tape. If you run over contour or fish worth investigating but happen not to be watching the finder, there it will all be, recorded on the tape. A disadvantage is that recorders, being somewhat more complicated machines, cost more.

RECORDER-FLASHER. Some units offer both kinds of readout. They keep a tape and also show the signals on a flasher face. A switch allows selectivity to one or the other or both. If you do a great deal of fishing you can conserve tape until the moments of truth arrive. Additional tape costs in most fishing are negligible, however. A 50-foot roll costs about $8.

Generally speaking, flashers are more common in freshwater. Power drain is so slight that many models are available as battery-powered portable units. Since the transducer is not permanently mounted, it can be moved from boat to boat. Salt water with its greater depths employs the recorders more. These could be battery-powered but as far as I know none are and they must be wired into the boat's 12-volt system.

Accessories

There are several items that increase the use of finders. Any type can be bought with an alarm signal. If you enter waters with depths below a preset number, the alarm sounds to alert you to the fact and prevent running aground. Sounders can also be used to some extent in navigation. The contours of the bottom correspond with underwater features to tell you where you are. Another accessory is a flexible arm on which the transducer can be mounted so the signal can be "beamed" in any given direction to look for fish.

Dual mounts found on many bass boats aren't strictly accessories because you have two flasher units usually reading off a single transducer. The duals are a convenience. One flasher can be read from the piloting position while running the boat. The other face is read from either bow or aft position (usually the bow) while running the electric. This is so you can find your hotspot while on the gas outboard and keep over it on the electric.

Maintenance

Water is the greatest enemy of any electronics, despite relatively recent improvements in transistorized equipment. The drier you can keep them, the better they will respond. I bought a piece of flexible convertible window plastic at an autotop store and sewed up covers for my RDF, sounder, and CB. It stays dry and I can still see it. Spraying the works with CRC or its equivalent can do no harm. Touch connectors from time to time with an emery cloth to keep electrical flow easy. In water that has marine growth, the face of the transducer must be scrubbed regularly because growth on it will weaken and finally knock out the signal. Never paint the face with an antifouling paint.

Radios

The use of private radios that you can use to talk to your buddies — or call for help at sea — is changing radically and rapidly, especially in the marine area. Here's what's happening at a glance.

AM marine radios are discontinued. The familiar 150-watt-maximum marine radio with its emergency frequency of 2182 can no longer be licensed. Its use worldwide, however, is so great that Coast Guard stations continue to monitor it.

Citizen's Band AM radio (CB radio) has increased from twenty-three to forty channels, and a new type greatly increases range and cost. The Coast Guard has recently announced plans to monitor CB channel 9.

The marine radio designed to replace AM marine is VHF/FM. It is now continuously monitored by all Coast Guard stations and ships.

Citizen's Band

One out of every forty cars on the road today has a CB radio, one of eight recreational vehicles. An estimated 500,000 CB units are in boats. Here are CB basics. Cost is reasonable. Fairly good hand-held "walkie-talkies" run as low as $75. Low-cost, forty-channel sets start in the $100 range, and the best cost around $300, including antenna. CB does not need a ground plate or tuning by a licensed technician. Most models can be easily transferred from boat to car, camp, camper, snowmobile, trailer, although you will probably need different antennas. Sets operate either on 12 volts or 115 (house current) and can be easily converted from one to the other. The FCC has designated channel 9 as the emergency channel, and in many areas of the country this is monitored continuously by bait stores, boat liveries, some police departments, fire and first aid squads, and now the Coast Guard. Holler into channel 9 night or day in this country and chances are somebody will hear you. FCC CB set licensing is free, and no operator's license is required.

CB's deficiencies are lack of range, static, and overcrowding of channels. Range is determined by antenna height; the higher the antenna the greater the range. Transmission on land is "line of sight"; on water a waterborne "ground" wave will increase range slightly. Mountains and buildings effectively block transmission. Range will vary depending on the above factors and also on how "peaked" transmitting and receiving sets are and sometimes on atmospheric conditions. Certain effective range is probably around 15 miles or less. Over water with equipment in top shape you can probably go 30 miles if you can find a channel unobstructed by other transmission.

Because it operates in the relatively high AM frequencies, CB picks up interference from engine electrical fields. Inboards, stern-drives, and outboards must be shielded. Suppressor spark plugs must be used. (New CB ignition "gap" plugs are available with suppressors.) Alternator and generator noise must be shielded and filtered, as must distributor noise. Inboard interference is worse than outboard, where thick cowls and distance reduce the interference.

Suppression equipment is not cheap. You can quickly spend $100. Nor is it uncomplicated. Unless you know something about what you are doing you'll need some help. Of course, you can always turn the engine off when you want to transmit or receive. Fortunately in a car, the metal firewall effectively seals out engine interference. CB is affected by sky-wave interference and skip. Especially at night you can often get Cuban fishing boats hundreds of miles away. In Puerto Rico recently they regularly talked with Australia.

Another less-well-known CB fact is that a licensed radio technician can usually tune a set better than the factory-pretuned version. What is done is that the exact transmitting characteristics of that set are matched with the exact characteristics of that antenna. Effective range can be increased this way 10 to 15 percent.

Overcrowding and misuse of the airways is the curse of the CB. Although required by law to limit conversations to five minutes, people chatter aimlessly forever about nothing. Commercial fishermen, especially shrimpers, are the ultimate worst. Bored to oblivion on their endless trawls, they blanket the airwaves, even sing into the transmitter, and take special delight in screaming obscenities at anyone who dares to tell them to shut up.

Single-Sideband CB

A relatively new form of CB, *second generation CB*, involves taking transmission off both sides of the radio wave (band is the correct word) and putting both bands on one. This single-sideband (SSB) effectively quadruples power. It also causes a more static-free signal since there is only half as much outside interference. Range is greatly increased as well. You can expect to double or triple range. Some SSB is compatible with regular CB—that is, the two can talk to one another. Other sets do not have this feature and can transmit to and receive only other SSB-equipped sets. SSB CB utilizes the same forty channels as regular CB, with channel 9 the emergency channel. SSB CB is expensive. Sets cost around $450 with antenna. Because its range is only slightly greater than new VHF/FM and it costs more, it would appear that anyone who is dissatisfied with regular CB should go to VHF/FM rather than SSB CB for boat use.

Very High Frequency FM

The marine radio designed to replace AM marine is Very High Frequency FM (VHF/FM), also called Ultra High Frequency FM (UHF/FM), and is sometimes written simply as VHF or UHF.

There are some excellent qualities to this radio. Because of the low frequency, it is as static free as your FM radio. Sky-wave interference is minimal. Dawn and dusk periods send AM sets crazy, but not FM. No ground plate is required. Little or no suppression of plugs, points, and so forth is needed. Over seventy channels have been designated. All Coast Guard stations and boats on patrol (and I believe now aircraft) continuously monitor channel 16, the calling and distress channel. The telephone company marine operators have been VHF/FM-equipped, so it is possible to connect by radio to land telephone networks at a cost of about $5.00 for a call under 300 miles and $10 beyond that. Another positive feature of VHF/FM is that it automatically receives the twenty-four–hour continuous weather broadcasts on 156.6 MHz. Yet another blessing is that all sets are required to have a switch so transmission can be at 1-watt power. When two skippers are discussing the weather across the marina, this low-power transmission will avoid interference with others.

However, the bad features of VHF/FM are real ones. First is cost. Costs have come down, but sets range from $350 to $800. Second is short range. It transmits only on line-of-sight, like your television set. Some Coast Guard stations are mounting antennas on 1,400-foot towers to extend range. In a sailboat or sportfisherman where high antenna mounts are possible, range in the 20- to 40-mile area can be expected. In an outboard where a 10-foot antenna presents problems enough, 8 miles might be the extreme distance over which two so-equipped boats could communicate. (The Coast Guard says range is 10–30 miles boat to land, 5–15 miles boat to boat.)

I might interject at this point that in physical size both types—CB and

VHF/FM — are similar, now little larger than an oversized cigar box. Power requirements for both transmitting and receiving are practically negligible if your boat has any kind of generating capability.

ESSA Weather

A fair amount of cities (thirty-two at last count) are now within range of twenty-four–hour weather reports put out by the ESSA. This is really good stuff, is updated constantly, often has tidal info, and gives readings from various locations. As stated, all VHF sets are equipped to receive this weather. In addition, smaller, battery-powered sets can be had that also pick it up. If you are boating within earshot of ESSA, by all means add one to your boat.

Aviation Weather

Less known but much more widely offered are twenty-four–hour continuous aviation weather forecasts. There are over 250 broadcast originations, and the radio has long-range AM characteristics. You should be able with a battery set to receive signals 100 or more miles away. Your local airport can give you info about this weather service.

Installation

There is no trick to installing either VHF or CB. If you put both aboard your boat, as many do, they can be coupled through the same antenna. Any dry spot, as shock free as possible, is a good spot for the radio. Most console boats have a space under the console for the radio. On a console boat you can mount the antenna on the side deck. Another good spot is on top of the windshield railing.

Radio Direction Finders

Radio direction finders (RDF) are a useful safety item aboard boats that go to sea in waters where fogs are regular. What the units do is give you a bearing to a specific signal, if possible two or more for a crossbearing fix. All are battery powered. The higher the price, the more sensitive the bearing. The disadvantage to them is the low power of most signals — 10 to 15 miles. This is okay if you are picking up a coastal inlet jetty but not good enough to find wrecks far offshore. Most sets function as AM/FM radios and can be used to add music and news to the ship. Most today include a band to receive ESSA weather as well.

14

Different Boats for Different Folks

What happens when two skippers with very definite ideas about things buy the same boat? Answer: They customize both to get exactly what they want. This is the story of those two boats. One is mine. The other belongs to a friend. First, my vessel, *Sports Afield Wanderer III*.

A Boat for the Bay

A while back I moved to the shores of Chesapeake Bay. To sample some of its fabled fishing required naturally a realigning of the Taylor fleet. The flagship, a cabin cat-boat, was sold. And I started on what finally resulted in an eighteen-month study project before I found and rigged a new vessel to my tastes. I measure the amount of research on stories by the height the paper pile reaches. Getting my boat was by no means the largest pile ever, but at the end it did reach at least 8 inches of letters, catalogues, and (ugh) bills and receipts. Here's what I did and why.

The best-riding boat I ever experienced is the 20-foot Bertram. Its deep-V hull takes rough water magnificently. The boat performs neatly on turns, rides beautifully at slow speeds, and has surprising stability at rest. However, this vessel is not made in an outboard version, and I didn't want the extra weight, corrosion problems, and explosion danger of inboard-outboard.

However, the second deep-V that Ray Hunt, its inventor, designed after the Bertram was originally built by Alum in a 17-foot outboard version. I'd seen two of these boats in action — wild action, as a matter of fact — and they were matchless. Wellcraft bought the molds from the defunct Alum and produces the boat in a 20-foot version.

Thus it was hull design and performance I had experienced myself that led me to this vessel. As far as the builder went, although I never personally inspected the Wellcraft plant, I've been through enough similar builder's plants to know that top-line builders use wholly satisfactory methods — that is, boats by one good builder will be

146

much like those of another insofar as workmanship and material are concerned. Well-craft enjoys a fine reputation. And I took the trouble to personally inspect several sister ships and liked what I saw. Here were well-built, rough-water vessels. What's more, I liked their looks. I enjoyed the sheer, the flaring bow to throw spray, the curve of her sides. I could (and do) stand back and feast my eyes on her.

At 20 feet, the boat offered ample cockpit fishing room, and a fully loaded weight of 2,750 pounds was easily trailerable. She would be a snap to load and launch with a power winch and tilt-bed trailer. I got a four-wheel trailer that made it simple to balance the boat's weight, and to forestall corrosion problems in the salt water where the boat will spend her life, I paid a premium price for an aluminum trailer. I must say that I am astonished at how easily the boat tows. Inertially activated brakes (on front axles only — about 85 percent of braking power comes from the front axle and 90 percent of the problems with brakes occurs on the back axle) give me excellent control with a mid-sized Buick wagon. I don't do any tailgating, though, and I'm super-cautious about passing.

As with so many popular hulls, Wellcraft offers this boat in both console and windshield configurations. For me, there was no hesitation. Disliking cold and wet, I want a top to get under and windshield to hide behind. Side and aft curtains really button her up. I found that the top was designed to fold and furl across the transom. Unshippy. This got quickly changed, so the top goes up over the windshield and the cockpit is open to ladle fish aboard. To catch the sun and keep cool, I furl the top and sit on the back of the helmsman's seat. It's somewhat easier to cast from a console boat, but with the hatch to the cuddy cabin open, one man can cast there, another atop the helm seat,

Smart styling of deep V shows on turn.

and a third aft. Not the best arrangement, to be sure, but this balances against the cuddy that makes a dry place to mount the electronics and store gear. There are two bunks, but for midgets only. A feature I *didn't* like was that there was no door to the cuddy. I had to rig a plywood panel, which I covered with Formica so I could close off and lock the cabin. To stow this underway I bolted two brackets made from flat aluminum stock under the deck forward. A shockcord line keeps the panel in place.

I powered her with a 135-hp Evinrude. (She came before the 200s were announced or I would have had one on her.) Why Evinrude instead of Chrysler or Merc? Certainly no mechanical reason. Frankly, I like the blue colors and over the years I have fished a lot with Evinrude guys. The 135 gives me a top speed fully loaded in the mid-30s, and at 3,800-rpm speeds in the upper 20s with a gallons-per-hour of about 8. This speed returns my greatest miles per gallon of about 3.8. Twin aluminum 20-gallon saddle tanks give me a range in excess of 100 miles, and being the cautious type I carry a 6-gallon can of gas as well. (By the way, as I have already explained, don't buy a new boat that doesn't have an aluminum gas tank. New alloys make these as good as Monel at prices only slightly higher than steel.) I put on an OMC fuel filter downline from a T valve so I can draw out of first one tank, then the other, and keep her trim. (By herself she'll run one tank dry, then suck air.) Most every time I gas up I pour a couple of shot glasses of rubbing alcohol into the tank to take out the water. I've never been a two-motor fan, preferring to take super loving care of one machine. However, I must admit my research for an article on twin powering taught me that the efficiency loss with twin outboards is nowhere near as great as with twin conventional motors. And for somewhere over $1,000 or $1,500, there is (rigged properly) the oh-so-nice dependability of twins.

Power Trim was another desired item (certainly not a must, however). With the boat right on level, the SST wheel provides maximum revs of about 4,500–4,600 rpm. Lower the bow for rough water and this drops several hundred rpm. In quiet water I lift the bow and the boat comes in exactly at 5,000 rpm, which is its rated max.

I mounted full OMC instruments: tach, battery condition and charging indicator, temperature gauge, gas gauges, speedometer. The dash is hard to mount a compass on. I put an OMC compass in the dash, but it is close enough to the tach (6 inches) to be affected, and I mounted a 4-inch Richie on the panel below the wheel. It is lit for night running. I have two top-quality preserver vests that stow under the back-to-back seats and two Gentex PVC foam preservers that just fit into a deck well in front of the windshield. Again, shock lines keep them in place. I built compartmented shelves on the sides of the cuddy and in a burst of genius made the faces out of Plexiglas so you can find the stuff in them quickly. Since I frequently run and fish at night, I put a dome light in the cuddy and mounted a compact 110,000-candlepower Guest handheld spot where I can reach it from the helm. It really blasts out, too. Horn is a Freon can to satisfy the fuzz. Bosch wipers clean the helmsman's window. Since the hull is not self-bailing, I mounted an automatic Lovett bilge pump in the drain well aft. All instruments come to a fuse panel behind the wheel.

The boat comes with a helmsman's seat to starboard and a back-to-back recliner to port. I debated throwing this out and installing another helmsman or even fashioning

Stern shot shows coolers, small cabinet on starboard side, riggers, and top that can be completely closed in.

a seat that doubled as a storage cabinet. I finally decided I could achieve ample storage space in other ways and the recliner would be a good place for me to lie down if I ever got seasick. The hull hasn't flotation, but there are two live wells under the cockpit sole. So far they've only been used to store beer.

For electronics I went to a Johnson twenty-three–channel CB with Antenna Specialists stainless antenna. A Ray Jeff recording-flasher depthsounder mounted in the cuddy but where I can see it from the wheel shows me fish, and with transducer aft flush-mounted with the bottom and spaces sealed with GE silicone caulk it reads at planing speeds. A Ray Jeff RDF is held in a special box just inside the cuddy. This is the least expensive RDF I know of, and it hasn't much sharpness on weak signals. I use it mostly for a weather radio. I was afraid spray would get under the cuddy, and as I mentioned in the preceding chapter I bought some clear plastic that I sewed together to fashion covers for the electronics. They didn't win the sewing bee but do a nice job. I mounted a high-tensile Danforth on the forward deck and carry 200 feet of 5/16-inch nylon in the forward rope locker. A Winchester flare gun stows forward. One large and two small fenders stow out of the way under the deck of the cuddy. My toolbox is complete. I stow tools in a cheap plastic tackle box minus the tray. I sawed a hammer handle so a regular-size hammer could fit it, found a small hacksaw that fit, have good pliers, several screwdrivers, files (hardest to keep from being ruined by rust), hand drill and bits, complete open-end wrench set, a couple adjustable wrenches, small pipe wrench, and so forth. I spray everything on the boat once a week — stainless rails, windshield rod holders, everything except lures — with CRC or WD-40. And I take out the tools and spray them too.

I wanted outriggers mostly for the salty way they look but also so I could on occasion fish four rods. Mine have 5-foot poles and operate manually into the up or down position. I mounted two flush rod holders in the side deck ahead of the tanks and two T-mounts on the inner gunwales aft where the saddle tanks forked them. Mostly I fish two rods out of these, Garcia Mitchell 622 reels with matched rods. These have proved just right for the 4- to 12-pound bluefish that fill the bay. I carry a Fenwick popping rod with 6000C Ambassador rigged and ready to cast to any breaking fish that attack me.

Storing fish and storing tackle are always tough in any small boat, and I solved this problem rather neatly, I think. I got two 84-quart Igloo chests, each 33 × 16 × 16 inches, that fit on both sides of the cockpit against the gas-tank panels. These make a good place to sit while trolling. One box serves as the fish box, and with blues you need one. The other box serves as storage for tackle and lures that are stowed in large transparent plastic boxes that apparently keep the stuff dry and relatively salt free since corrosion hasn't been a problem.

There it is — a boat for the bay. While outfitting her was fun, it was also expensive. And there was a tear or two amid the sunshine. I must say, though, that it came out okay. She's a real running little bucket.

Oh, the bill? I figure the cost to duplicate the boat today would run between $9,000 and $11,500.

Same Boat—Different Customizing

Claude Rogers' job requires him to fish almost every day, and no one knows the inlets and bays of Virginia's famed barrier-island chain better than he does. For years a little 17-foot deep-V Alum aided him in the pursuit of striped bass, blues, white marlin, black drum, and, most of all, channel bass. However, after ten years of hard use the Alum was wearing thin. It was time for a new version.

Sticking with a proven performer, Claude also opted for the 20-foot Wellcraft version of the same deep-V hull. He liked the soft riding characteristics. For him, a forward deck was a must for the dry storage area it created. The Wellcraft's flared bow turns spray beautifully.

However, the shape and configuration was the only thing Claude wanted from the manufacturer. He ordered the boat stripped! No tanks, no seats, no hardware. Only the windshield came with the boat. He wouldn't trust anyone even to use the right kind of cleats. He demanded complete control over each and every item that went on his vessel. And as soon as he took delivery, off went the boat to a boat customizer for extensive revisions.

First to go was the afterdeck, the floor of the boat. This was sawed out and a well built to take four 6-gallon outboard gas tanks. The standard saddle tanks took up too

In Claude's boat the space between windshield and Bimini top allows free circulation of air. Note the flaring sides that throw spray.

much room in Claude's view. The next customizing was the addition of a huge splash well in front of the outboard. Claude uses his well to keep bait in and to hold large fish covered with a wet burlap bag. The well also serves as a catchall for empty bottles, place to wash waders, and so forth. He positions a fold-down step on the transom to make it easy, even wearing waders, to step on this step, then into the well, and finally into the boat itself. The forward deck of the well is 6 inches wide, so it is comfortable to sit on.

When the boat's floor was open, Claude had the boat fully filled with PVC foam. This added less than 25 pounds and completely damped the noise of the boat going through the water.

The next customizing touches were a compartmentalized series of bins that run along the starboard side from the helmsman's seat all the way aft. These are approximately 6 inches wide, 6 inches deep, and 5 inches long. They can be covered with tops and locked. The bins hold surf-fishing sinkers, pliers, corks, signal markers, knives, wires, and fishing gear.

Claude accepted the manufacturer's windshield but backed out all the screws that held it in place and replaced them with bolts. (I did the same thing.) He declined the bow rail, which is really only to prevent you from falling overboard when anchoring. In this boat the windshield hatch slides forward to accommodate anchoring, so the rail is really more for cosmetic purposes than anything else (and at approximately $250 it had better be beautiful).

Another innovation of this skipper was a Bimini top but rigged *not* to attach to the top of the windshield as is customary. Instead there is about a 3-inch gap so underway a good circulation of air is forced down behind the windshield. This top folds on the deck in front of the windshield for storage. (While Claude's top arrangement is great for hot-weather work, in cold and/or wet weather my all-button-up windshield is warm and cozy. Opening the center panel of the windshield gives me all the ventilation I need.)

Rod holder went on. Four flush-mounts went into side decks. This was possible here because the lack of saddle tanks permitted them. Another was mounted on the windshield so a rod could be kept instantly available to cast to a fish. A single chrome-on-brass cleat went on the forward deck, and two went aft. They are through-deck-bolted with four 1/2-inch bolts with oversize washers to 1/2-inch plywood backing plates.

A seatbox was made out of plywood and fiberglassed. It was positioned so that sitting in a spring-shocked Pompanette captain's seat Claude can see over the top of the windshield through the top gap when salt spray obscures the windshield. Inside the seat is more storage. The other seat is a standard Pompanette back-to-back. Another 6-gallon can of gas is stored under it as a reserve tank.

Instruments for the Johnson 135 are speedometer and tachometer. A Konel recorder is mounted on the dash right in front of the helmsman's eyes. A Unimetric CB completes the electronics. An Aquameter compass is mounted on a windshield support that puts it under the helmsman's eye, also.

Auxiliary power is by a 35-hp Johnson on a bracket aft. This also makes a good shallow-water powerplant because the prop turns in the area of the V and is only an inch lower than the extreme depth of the keel.

To facilitate night fishing, dome lights are mounted on both sides of the cockpit under decks so that items can be easily seen but no light shines on the water to scare fish.

So that's it — two very different boats that started as the same hull. And there's a third version — the one you really should be thinking about: the one that's right for *you*.

To solve the compass mount, Claude rigged his on the windshield support. I put on an OMC flush mount on the dash and Richie about knee height on panel below wheel.

Index